Dr Nic Hooper is an expert in clin
senior lecturer at the University of the West of
in Bristol. He has authored many scientific articles,
book chapters and books, including *The Acceptance and
Commitment Diary* (published annually) and *The Research
Journey of Acceptance and Commitment Therapy*. Nic is also
a co-director of Connect, which is an organisation that offers
a psychological wellbeing curriculum for primary school
children. In 2017, inspired by his students, Nic began to write
a book of life advice to his son, Max, which was to be given to
him on his eighteenth birthday. Over time, that book slowly
transformed into *The Unbreakable Student*.

More praise for *The Unbreakable Student*

'Nic Hooper has pulled off a neat trick for a professor, essentially creating a long-form lecture that remains engaging and informative to the very end. Equal parts practical, funny and illuminating, *The Unbreakable Student* belongs on the required reading list for life. Young people everywhere are lucky to have him, in person or on the page'

— **Sarah Knight, internationally bestselling
author of *Get Your Sh!t Together***

'Going to university is a tumultuous time in any case, but this is doubly true when there's a pandemic happening. Hooper's new guide couldn't be timelier. Drawing on many years of relevant experience and training, it's a must for any student beginning this next stage of their life'

— **Dean Burnett, neuroscientist and
author of *The Idiot Brain***

'Going to university is a fantastic opportunity that can transform students' lives, but we also know it throws up many new challenges. *The Unbreakable Student* is a very well-written and researched companion, with valuable tools, tips and techniques that will help students deal with these challenges and make the most of their journey. I would recommend it to all students studying at university – and to their parents too'

— Professor Steven West, Vice-Chancellor at the University of the West of England, and Chair of the Universities UK Mental Health in Higher Education Working Group

'What a useful guide for students! It's raw, authentic, personal, soulful, entertaining and pragmatic. In my opinion, this is a must-have for young adults in higher education'

— Scott Barry Kaufman, psychologist and author of *Transcend: The New Science of Self-Actualization*

'Nic's guide to staying sane at university is full of solid, sensible advice, delivered with a smile and a side helping of science. Nic doesn't just tell you what to do, he tells you why and gives you a whole range of ideas about how. In truth, I wish this book had existed for me to read during my own university adventure'

— Pooky Knightsmith, author and international expert in child and adolescent mental health

'Nic Hooper has written such a timely and powerful book! People in this stage of life may feel unseen, confused, over-whelmed and unsure about how to meet their emotional needs. Hooper understands this deeply, and provides them with identification, a caring voice and a road map to resilience and health'

— Jonathan Hoban, psychotherapist and author of *Walk with Your Wolf*

THE UNBREAKABLE STUDENT

6 RULES FOR STAYING SANE AT UNIVERSITY

DR NIC HOOPER

ILLUSTRATIONS BY JOHN-PAUL FLINTOFF

ROBINSON

ROBINSON

First published in Great Britain in 2021 by Robinson

A CIP catalogue record for this book is available from the British Library

ISBN: 978-1-47214-539-0

Typeset in Sentinel by Initial Typesetting Services, Edinburgh
Printed and bound in Great Britain by Clays Ltd, Elcograf S.p.A.

Papers used by Robinson are from well-managed forests and other responsible sources

MIX
Paper from
responsible sources
FSC® C104740

Robinson
An imprint of
Little, Brown Book Group
Carmelite House
50 Victoria Embankment
London EC4Y 0DZ

An Hachette UK Company
www.hachette.co.uk

www.littlebrown.co.uk

To my wife Amy, my son Max, my dog Dora and to the students I've been lucky enough to work with over the years.

Contents

Chapter 1

What You Need to Know Before We Start

Sarah's story

I want you to imagine an eighteen-year-old sitting in their university room. Imagine them hunched over their desk. Imagine tears slowly rolling down their face because of how overwhelmed they feel.

This scene hasn't been fabricated to build drama: I've seen it with my own eyes. I was called late one night to the room of a student who was considering suicide. When I arrived, *Sarah* was shaking and crying. She told me that she couldn't make her negative thoughts and feelings go away. In her eyes, life wasn't worth living any longer. Those words easily roll off the tongue, but that night I was looking into the eyes of another human being who felt so low that she no longer wanted to exist.

I'd like to say this was unusual, but since that particular incident I've spoken to other students

whose self-worth is broken enough that they too
have considered what Sarah was considering.

Unfortunately, my experiences mirror what's
happening in the wider world. There has been an
epidemic in student suicides recently; governmen-
tal task forces have discovered that one in three
students suffers from a mental health problem;
and scientific articles suggest that less than half of
the student population report good psychological
wellbeing. These findings have made their way
into numerous stories in the media. When people
read of such developments, it's probably easy to feel
distanced from the human beings who make up the
numbers. In my line of work, I don't get that luxury. I
see students struggle. I could see Sarah struggling.

Around two hours later Sarah was sat up, holding
a cup of coffee and telling me about her life. Sarah
was a person, rich in experience and wisdom, and
someone who was so much more than her unwanted
thoughts and feelings. I just needed her to see it. I
needed her to see possibilities. But what should I say?

Hi everybody! (said in the voice of Dr Nick from *The Simpsons*)

Before we go on, it feels important to introduce myself. My name is Dr Nic Hooper (some people call me *Dr Nic*, some people call me *Hoopdog*, you can call me *Nic*), and I work at the University of the West of England as a psychology lecturer and researcher. Picture a middle-aged white guy (because not enough of them are writing books), with scruffy brown hair and a non-designer beard, wearing a tweed jacket, glasses with a thick black rim, and speaking with an accent that you can't quite put your finger on. I grew up in Wales (that's a different country from England for those North Americans among you) and attended a good school. My father was a window cleaner and my mother was a primary school secretary by day and a gymnastics teacher by night. We lived in a poor area because, frankly, we were a poor family. But my parents gave me everything they could (love, support and money) and they pushed me to view the world as my oyster. After moving through the education system, I eventually went to Swansea University to study psychology. Seven years later, I left Swansea with a degree and a PhD (and a shedload of debt).

In August 2010, I moved to England to work as a post-doctoral researcher at the University of Kent. However, my dream was to work abroad. By February 2011, I was applying for jobs everywhere and was fortunate enough to be offered the role of Assistant Professor at Middle East Technical University (their Northern Cyprus Campus). My partner at the time (Amy, who's now my wife) and I saw Northern Cyprus as an opportunity to have an adventure (little did we know how much of an adventure it would turn out to be – I'll tell you more about that later on). After eighteen months abroad, we returned to the UK (with a former street dog, Dora), got married, and had a baby (Max). Most of you probably don't have children, but one day you'll discover that it's an experience equal in vulnerability and joy.

We'll come to know each other more throughout this book but I wanted to give you some of my history early on, to show you that I'm not a distant and aloof psychology professor with no understanding of the struggles of every-day people. I'm a *real* human being who has lived through many of the experiences that *normal* people live through, and fifteen years ago I wouldn't have been too different from who you are right now.

What's this book about?

This book is your blueprint for optimal psychological health. In order to achieve this, the chapters map onto the *Six Ways to Wellbeing*, a framework first introduced by Dr Geetanjali Basarkod. Through multiple studies, Dr Basarkod showed that there are six behaviours that psychologically healthy people tend to do a lot. If you want top-notch wellbeing, you should:

1. Exercise

2. Challenge yourself

3. Connect with others

4. Give to others

5. Practise self-care

6. Embrace the moment

The point of this book, therefore, is quite simple: to get you doing those things more often. However, there's a catch, which makes this task not quite so simple. It doesn't take a genius to understand that those six behaviours will probably be useful for human beings, and yet most of us don't do them. Why? Well, our minds get in the way. The psychological make-up of human beings is complex and can impact our ability to bring those *Six Ways to Wellbeing* to life. Consequently, in addition to exploring one way to wellbeing in each chapter, I'll also be talking about some useful ways of dealing with our thoughts and feelings.

A map of this book

In summary then, this book is made of six main chapters that will give you the psychological skills to engage in the most important wellbeing behaviours for human beings. Given my occupation, you could visualise those chapters as a series of lectures (the really amazing kind of face-to-face lecture rather than the dull online ones that you'll no doubt have to endure at some point in this post-Covid-19 world). Think Robin Williams in *Good Will Hunting* (if you haven't watched that movie because it was born in the '90s then I'd urge you to put aside your reservations – you'll thank me later).

Anyhow, I'll set the scene to get you in the mood for this opening chapter. Picture me at the front of a university hall, with two hundred students bustling into their seats. The students vary in what they wear (some look like hippies and some are dressed in semi-formal attire) and some of them definitely smell of a hangover. The seats are old, rickety and brown. You're in the audience, near the middle and therefore quite high up, possibly sitting next to someone that you rather fancy but haven't told yet (my gut says this happens all the time). You open your laptop ready to make notes and you see me lift up my right hand. The classroom falls silent. You then notice an outrageous thought pop into your head, *'Wow, what a good-looking man that lecturer is.'* You feel a little weird about having the thought, but luckily that feeling is interrupted when I say the famous words of any self-indulgent academic, *'I'll begin.'*

Have you noticed how happy dogs are?

OK – that subhead might have thrown you – so it feels important to put in a disclaimer here. In these early pages, the information I present may seem like the incoherent ramblings of a buffoon, but I promise you that it all leads somewhere. You see, before we get into your blueprint for good psychological health, we need to talk first about what bad psychological health is and how it happens. Here goes.

Every so often, I sit on the sofa, see my dog in her bed, and think that I'd hate to be a pet. I mean, what's there to do? Staying inside for most of the day, going for a little walk and being fed dog food would be bad enough, but imagine just lying around a lot of the time, not achieving anything, life basically amounting to diddly-squat. I respect Dora Hoopdog, because if I were her, I think I'd be depressed. But she isn't. When I feed her, walk her or smooth her, she wags her tail in a way that makes me think she's happy. In fact, when she settles down for an afternoon snooze, it's impossible for me to describe just how happy she looks, wrapped up with a blanket, in front of the fire, surrounded by her bones.

Yes, I spoil my Dora, but I want to draw your attention to something curious. You and I, in all likelihood, already have what Dora has. Nope, I don't mean brown fur, a bed under the stairs or an affinity for chasing squirrels. I mean that we exist in a world where our basic needs are met (food, shelter, love and warmth). For Dora, having those needs met is enough.

Have you noticed how happy human beings are?

My experience is that toddlers tend to be much the same as dogs. Sometimes, I wish I could return to my childhood and look around. I think I'd have been a lot like Dora. For example, when lining up my Thomas the Tank Engines, eating pancakes, watching TV and visiting grandparents, I would have been a happy little sausage. Don't get me wrong – I'd have been unhappy every now and then (for example, when my brother kicked the Thomas the Tank Engine lines across our living room) – but these experiences would have been short-lived. What I'm saying is that, in my eyes, a toddler is a less hairy, less smelly (sometimes) and slightly angrier version of a dog. Give them food, shelter, love and warmth and they're generally happy.

However, soon this all changes. While dogs continue to live contentedly, human beings gradually lose their grip on this thing that we call *happiness*. This happens because although dogs and toddlers can be the same in certain respects (how little they listen to me being another major similarity), in other ways they're very different. Specifically, from around three to five years old, children develop cognitive abilities that are far beyond the abilities of any dog that has ever existed. Yes, even Marley (*Marley And Me*), Baxter (*Anchorman*), Samantha (*I Am Legend*), Max (*How The Grinch Stole Christmas*) and Pit Bull (*John Wick*) aren't as smart as your average four-year-old human being.

These newfound cognitive abilities, and the development of language in particular, allow younger children to do many things, three of which are notable when it comes to happiness:

- Firstly, **they now understand that they have their own minds** (and can make their own decisions) and that other people have minds that are separate from their own.

- Secondly, this theory of mind (that's what it's called in the psychological literature) makes them **more aware of their own thoughts and feelings**. While dogs continue with their daily routines, children develop the ability to recognise and label their own emotions, and the emotions of others.

- Thirdly, **children can now time-travel**. That is, they can remember times when they've felt happy, or predict times when they might be happy, and compare it to the feelings they experience in the here and now.

Our cognitive abilities continue to develop from toddlerhood (I'm not convinced that's a word but I'm going with it nonetheless), to childhood and right through adolescence into adulthood, and they're supremely useful. For example, these abilities are probably the reason why human beings are the dominant species on this planet: language has allowed us to work together to overcome threats from animals that are stronger, faster and more appropriately equipped for hunting than us (e.g. sharper teeth and claws).

Think about it. Human beings are pretty rubbish physically when compared to other animals, but we have the key to the world because of the fact that one human being can say to another, *'You go this way, I'll go that way, you distract the sabre-toothed tiger by flossing* [the dance rather than practising good dental hygiene], *and then I'll shoot this arrow into his head.'* In fact, the greatest achievements in the history of mankind have happened only as a result of our advanced cognitive abilities (think of controlling fire, the pyramids, the steam train, music, literature, walking on the moon and, of course, the umbrella hat).

However, the unfortunate thing about these cognitive abilities is that they also allow us to get better and better at comparing, analysing, remembering, imagining, predicting, judging, reflecting and mind-reading, which are skills that are likely to be at the heart of psychological troubles. And this, regrettably for us human beings, is why happiness is a feeling we'll struggle to keep hold of.

It gets worse ...

But that's not the end of the story. The kick in the teeth here is that, over time, our struggle with happiness will be made even harder by the nature of life. To paraphrase *Forrest Gump* (another great '90s movie you should watch if you haven't already), whether we like it or not, shit happens. I was reminded of this recently when taking a jog down memory lane. A good friend of mine lost his dad suddenly when he was young. I remember it. I remember the hurt that jumped out of his eyes. He reacted with strength, which no doubt helped his lovely mother and his younger sisters. This strength grew in him. He continued to care for various members of his family and played rugby to a high standard. Then, when he was just about to begin university, his mother was diagnosed with an inoperable brain tumour. She died four weeks later. I saw him shortly after the funeral in a pub. While I sat opposite him, his face said nothing. It was numb. At such a young age, my friend had no father, no mother and two sisters to look after.

When I think of that friend a chill runs down my spine. To think of the psychological pain that he has endured really gets to me. However (and I would never say this to him because of how hurtful it might sound), his pain is far from uncommon. His story is one of a million stories just like it. I would go so far as to say that almost every person I know has experienced psychological pain of some kind due to the nature of life.

Whether they've lost a loved one, live with a physical ailment, have developed an addiction, find themselves in occupations that are unfulfilling or in situations where they feel they have no control, whether they're unhappy with their outward appearance, have broken contact with family members, have lived through a traumatic event, whether they happen to find themselves in the middle of a world-changing pandemic or whether they experience isolation or ostracism or failure or frustration or disappointment or exhaustion or injustice, or even if they grapple with spirituality and the meaning of life ... The list of psychologically draining experiences that human beings can go through is a pretty long one.

The silver lining

I know all of this isn't really an uplifting start to a book about positive psychological wellbeing, but there's good reason to talk about it. I tell you these things because I want you to have realistic expectations about the inner worlds of human beings. They can be dark places at times. Whether we like it or not, due to our cognitive abilities and due to the inevitably difficult nature of life, we'll spend much time swimming in the seas of sadness, guilt, anger, worry, anxiety, stress, paranoia, fear, shock and many other difficult emotions.

Crucially, given that we can't stop our complex cognitive abilities from developing and given that we can't stop the difficult nature of life, those emotions are absolutely normal for human beings. What I'm saying is that even though you may see lots of people walk around with the words *'I'm fine'* tattooed on their forehead, the truth is that if you struggle psychologically at some point in your life that won't make you part of the minority: it will make you part of the majority. It's important to pause and appreciate this fact when we get caught into thinking that we're abnormal for having mental health struggles.

People walk around with 'I'm Fine' on their forehead

Let me say this another way in the context of your context. Although university is painted to be all fun and games by people out there in the world, the truth is that it can be hard. You may be in a new or foreign environment, you may have tricky people to navigate your way around, you may have difficult assignments to put together under pressure, you may have the stress of exams, you may have to cook for yourself and manage your own finances, and you may have to do all of this while being away from your loved ones. It's a monumental transition. Therefore, if you ever go through some stuff during your university adventure, it'll be down to the fact that life has become a little harder, and not because there's any major abnormality inside you. In other words, you'll be experiencing totally normal emotions given the change in situation. Unwanted, yes – abnormal, no.

I'll just not think about it

However, the fact that it's normal to have anxious, worrisome and depressing thoughts and feelings at university (and in life more generally) tells us very little about what to do with them when they visit us. This issue is an important one to explore because if we do the wrong thing with these standard inner experiences then we can very quickly find ourselves in psychological trouble. The go-to strategy is avoidance; many of us will try to avoid our unwanted thoughts and feelings.

'Why?' I hear you ask. Well, unwanted thoughts and

feelings aren't nice, so it makes sense to try to get rid of them in the same way that we might try to avoid many things that aren't nice. Not only that, but we see the message of avoidance all around us. For example, when the people we know feel down or stressed they tend to drink alcohol, take drugs, gamble, have casual sex, isolate themselves, eat ludicrous amounts of ice cream or binge-watch Netflix. We see those behaviours and figure that that must be the way to manage unwanted thoughts and feelings.

Our history of avoidance

Arguably, however, a bigger contributor to the popularity of avoidance in our society comes from an interesting place – mainstream ideas about mental health. When we take a closer look, many mental health approaches have the basic aim of trying to help us to get rid of our unwanted thoughts and feelings. These approaches, which started a long time ago and continue to dominate the treatment of human suffering, view these unwanted thoughts and feelings as abnormal events (almost like viruses) that need to be gone before we can live a proper life. Let me give you a brief but fascinating history.

In the 1700s, Benjamin Rush (one of the chaps who signed the United States Declaration of Independence) helped people to avoid their psychological troubles with blisters, water therapies, purges, emetics, spinning therapy and the famous tranquilliser chair (if you're wondering why such treatments were used, it was because Rush guessed that mental health problems were caused by abnormalities in the blood vessels). Later on, physicians tried to help people avoid unwanted thoughts and feelings with cathartics, bloodletting and physical restraints like straitjackets and cribs (here, mental health problems were thought to be caused by worn-out nerves). If I'd lived in those days, I'd have been telling no one about the inner workings of my mind.

By the late 1800s, lesions in the brain and defective germ plasm were thought to cause mental health problems and in the early 1900s, our kidneys and livers became the prime suspects (hydrotherapy units were developed to help in this regard). Next, patients were injected with animal hormones and suffered horrific side effects as a result (here, hormonal glands were thought to be at the heart of psychological troubles). After this, a bunch of other explanations for mental health problems led to the development of more and more extravagant interventions. Physicians removed various parts of the human body (I'm not kidding, the most popular bits were the teeth and ovaries), patients were given malaria treatment, frozen treatment, insulin coma therapy and metrazol convulsive therapy.

Nowadays, it hasn't really got a whole lot better. For example, lobotomies (cutting out parts of people's brains) and electroconvulsive therapy (electrocuting people's brains) are still in use, both of which can have dire consequences for human functioning (these treatments assume that mental health problems are caused by brain abnormalities). Even many talking therapies and anti-depressants have the explicit aim of helping people to avoid feeling down or anxious or stressed (and they 'work' by correcting thinking patterns and by rebalancing chemical hormones respectively).

But has avoidance worked?

So, it makes sense that people view unwanted thoughts and feelings as abnormalities that need to be avoided. Intellectually, we don't want to stay in touch with things that we find distressing, and the message of avoidance is, and has always been, popular with both lay people and mental health experts. However – and this is the crucial thing to get from our walk through history – it might appear that the list of treatments I've just described, delivered over the course of a few hundred years, are very different, but they're tied together in three important respects:

1. None of the treatments has any real clue, or solid evidence, about what causes mental health problems in the first place. It might be unsettling to read that, but psychological and medical science just don't have an answer to this question yet.

2. Each approach involves trying to help people avoid thoughts they don't want to think and avoid feelings they don't want to feel. They each try to help people run away from their demons.

3. Whether the avoidance takes the shape of layman interventions (alcohol, drugs, isolation) or

professional interventions (lobotomy, ECT, anti-depressant drugs) none of them has really worked too well. That's a bold statement, I know, but if there were an approach that really worked, that reliably cured people of the unwanted thoughts and feelings that come with mental health problems, then mental health wouldn't be such an issue in modern-day society.

What not to do after you've been dumped

Psychological science puts forward a compelling account of why avoidance-based approaches may not work. Even though our experience tells us that we can solve problems by avoiding threatening stuff, avoidance of our thoughts and feelings isn't the same thing as the avoidance of danger out there in the real world. For example, if a hungry hippo is running through your university, then go and hide somewhere to avoid the danger. But what if that hippo actually represented depression, anxiety or worry, and what if he was running not through your university but through your own mind? Could you hide from your own mind? I doubt that you could, and I'd bet that the more you tried not to think about something the more you would come to think about it (there's oodles of research on *thought suppression* that supports this idea). What I'm saying is that the problem-solving strategy of avoidance, when applied to our unwanted thoughts and feelings, won't work, because the human mind is too complex to allow us to hide from our demons.

However, that won't stop us from trying, and this sentiment leads us to consider something else about avoidance: not only will it not work, but it can also make things worse.

The first way this happens involves how we avoid. Sometimes, we avoid in relatively harmless ways (exercise, watching TV, going for a dog walk) but sometimes we don't. For example, we might distract ourselves with a bunch of other things that do us no favours in the long term, some of which I listed earlier on. I'm sure it wouldn't take you long to think of a time when you did something stupid in an attempt to rid yourself of some unwanted thought or feeling (I'll never forget the hangover I had after my first dog died). And, of course, when we wake up in the morning, our problems come flooding back to us anyway.

The second way that we try to avoid is even more harmful. We soon learn that if we want to increase the chances of successfully escaping from certain feelings or thoughts then all we have to do is avoid situations where they're likely to occur. In other words, in order to avoid unwanted thoughts and feelings we tend to stop doing stuff, and this will take us further away from the sort of life we'd like to be living.

I'll give an example that in no way resembles an event from my own life. It definitely doesn't resemble an experience I had following a whirlwind holiday romance as a sixteen-year-old. Imagine going to the cinema is an activity that I like to do. One day I meet a lovely young girl who I fall in love with. We go to the cinema every Saturday (for the sake of the story let's say that our first film was *Coyote Ugly*). Then, one day, my honeybunch dumps me for an older boy who has a car, shattering my heart into little pieces, leaving me troubled, unhappy and sobbing uncontrollably. I really don't want to experience these feelings so in the weeks that follow I try to distract myself by playing computer games. A little bit of time goes past and I'm doing OK when I get a text from a friend asking me to go to the cinema with him. I immediately decline the invitation because going to the cinema will bring up the sadness and the pain that I've been trying to avoid. By doing this, I'm narrowing my life (in a way that can sometimes be almost unconscious or automatic), and as we can be reminded of painful experiences so easily, soon I'll have to avoid the world in order to avoid my feelings. If I do this then what sort of life would I be living? Not a great one (I'd assume).

I'll give you another example (again, this one isn't based on me, I promise). Imagine, like most people, I value friendship. I want to build relationships with people. Unfortunately, however, I feel I'm socially awkward. One day I'm invited to a party and I muster up the courage to go. On my way to the party, I start experiencing some awful feelings. I feel anxious, inadequate and imagine myself to be different from everyone else. If I want to avoid those feelings, then the easy way to do that is to turn around, go back to my room and watch Netflix. In doing so, despite feeling happier ('relieved' is probably a better word) immediately following the retreat, I would have moved away from something that mattered to me in the long term: making friends. My life would have narrowed as a result of the avoidance.

How this might play out at university

Those two scenarios are pretty good examples for you to think about given the stage of life you're at. Firstly, if you find yourself with a romantic partner at university and that relationship breaks down, would you let that event impact the things you do and the places you go? Would you avoid stuff to (1) avoid the discomfort of seeing your ex and (2) avoid the feelings of pain that certain places bring up in you? Secondly, university is a social environment and making friends is important. When you get invited on a night out with new people, there's every chance that you'll feel some anxiety about it – but would you avoid the event in order to avoid the anxiety?

As you can imagine, avoidance behaviours can play out at university in lots of other ways too, but let me describe the one that I find particularly common. Presentations. Research suggests that the most severe fear people have is public speaking. Do you know what comes in at number 2? Death. So, when you get asked to do a presentation in university, it's likely that every inch of your body will want to avoid it. What would you do? If you avoid the presentation then you'll avoid the anxiety-provoking activity, but if you avoid the anxiety-provoking activity then your life has become smaller.

Becoming a behaviour analyst (not like the kind in *Mindhunter*)

Given how avoidance can creep into our lives so easily, going forward it will be important to think about whether avoidance is powering some of your decisions. But how can you do this? Well, you can improve what a psychologist would call your *behaviour analysis* skills (sounds cool, right?). In other words, improve your ability to break down situations and figure out what's really going on. You'll obviously need to do this with a focus on your own behaviour in time, but you could start off practising on your friends (though be careful with this, as it will be a weird and uncomfortable interaction if they find out what you're doing).

I'll give you an example. Imagine that your friend Chloe arrives home from university, picks up the controller for the console and plays games all night. On the one hand, this behaviour might be perfectly acceptable – perhaps Chloe just loves spending her time doing this. On the other hand, something else could be going on. Perhaps she's been having trouble in university with a classmate, has come home and just wants to distract herself for a bit. Sometimes, it's easier to do this sort of thing than it is to deal with the world. She wakes up the next morning, goes to university, and realises that she has forgotten to complete an assignment. Is it possible that Chloe was trying to avoid feeling certain feelings or thinking certain thoughts by playing the game for hours? Is it possible that she avoided doing her assignment because it would remind her of the stress from university?

The trick is figuring out when avoidance is pushing someone around. When Harry comes home and listens to music for hours, is that happening because the activity is valued, or because he's trying not to think about something? When Narik gets drunk on cheap cider, why has he done that? The only way to determine what's going on in such situations is to talk to your friends and gather information. Then you must trust what your intuition says about why they're doing the things they're doing. If you suspect avoidance, is there a way to highlight the potential pitfalls of taking this approach?

If you can manage to do this type of behavioural analysis on your friends, then soon enough you'll be able to do it on yourself too. That is, you'll be able to spot how attempted avoidance of unwanted thoughts and feelings is prompting you to make decisions that aren't in your long-term interest, and that will be a wonderful skill for you to have.

The lecture finishes. I turn off the projector. I gather my things. I run back to my office and sit in a daze for seventeen minutes before getting on with the rest of my day.

The take-home

In my working life, students often ask me the following question, *'What's wrong with trying to get rid of our unwanted thoughts and feelings – surely that's how we*

can be happy?' And in response, they get the lecture that
I've just given to you. My hope is that they, and now you,
understand that happiness is not the default state of affairs
for human beings and that chasing it by trying to avoid
our unwanted thoughts and feelings is the quickest way to
psychological trouble. *'OK,'* I can imagine you saying with
a frustrated look on your face, *'but if not avoidance, then
what?'* Well, that's the purpose of this book. As I said at the
beginning of the chapter, I'm going to teach you about the
Six Ways to Wellbeing and about better ways of dealing
with your unwanted thoughts and feelings. And this nicely
brings me to my next point.

As you read the previous paragraph, I doubt that you
began to jump up and down with excitement. There's
at least a chance you didn't have the following thought,
'Wahoo, I can't wait to sink my teeth into this bad boy.'
I know that reading a book about psychological wellbeing
might not seem that important (chances are that you didn't
even buy this book yourself but instead were given it as a
gift by your parents, who are basically terrified of you being
in university by yourself), but let me try to convince you
that this endeavour will be worth your time.

Firstly, if you find yourself struggling at university, you'll
want to know your way around psychological wellbeing,
and **this book can be your guide**. However, I think I
can go one step further here. If you happen to be someone
who doesn't generally struggle psychologically, then this
book can still matter for you. You can use the information
within it to help your friends, you can use the information

within it as a protective tool for yourself, and you can use the information within it to move from a neutral wellbeing position to a place where you understand how to flourish in this game of life.

Secondly, **this book will not be dry**. There are plenty of word-heavy, preachy, turn-your-life-around type books written by people with great academic articulation. I'd rather stub my toe than write another one of those. Nope – this book will be entertaining. Seriously. I've been teaching students for over a decade now and I know how to make them laugh. I swear way too much, I call them out on their shenanigans, I point out deflection tactics when they don't know the answers, and my ability to recognise a hangover and play on it is something special to see. And before you tell me that my students probably laugh out of pity for an old man, I can assure you (1) that I'm not old (although my ever-growing bald patch might disagree), and (2) that their grades don't depend on them laughing at my jokes (most of the time).

Actually, this *being entertaining* thing is a truly important tool when I teach. Why? Because if my students feel entertained then they'll learn without even realising that they're learning. It's like a Jedi mind trick. This book will do that for you – you'll learn about how to achieve better psychological wellbeing without really knowing that I'm teaching you about it because you'll be entertained (unless you happen to be a fan of word-heavy-preachy-turn-your-life-around type books).

So, in short, take this journey with me. You won't regret it. One other thing: at the end of each chapter there are a couple of tasks for you to complete in your own time, which will illustrate some of the concepts I've taught you about. With that in mind, I hope you enjoy what follows.

Chapter 1 Tasks

Task 1 – Spotting avoidance

Whether it's depression, anxiety, stress, relationship troubles, anger, addiction, psychosis or worry, most people have psychological troubles at some point in their life, and most people employ avoidance tactics to deal with such troubles. In an ideal world, I want you to see this for yourself. To that end, next time you're in a conversation with someone who happens to be particularly unhappy, stressed or annoyed, I want you to take notes in your mind. Try to dig at:

- Why the unwanted feelings developed.

- How they tended to be dealt with.

- Whether such strategies were successful.

Quickly, you'll see the temporal sequence of events (the context that led to the unwanted thoughts and feelings, how they were managed, and the result of employing such an approach) and you'll see how avoidance, in its many forms, can be harmful.

Once you've had this conversation, I'd like you to record your thoughts about the experience of doing this task (and your thoughts about this chapter more generally) on the notes page of your smartphone.

Save this page with the knowledge that we're going to keep updating it throughout the book. Of course, if you're *old skool,* then feel free to etch your thoughts onto a stone, or write them into a paper journal instead, whatever works.

Task 2 – Giving avoidance a try

There's a story written by Leo Tolstoy (he was a famous Russian writer) about two brothers. I can't remember the exact details, so I'll tell the story how I hope it happened. The older brother, somewhat annoyed by the little brother (probably after years of having his Thomas the Tank Engine lines kicked all over the living room), wanted to figure out a way to stop him from being such a pain. He called his little brother over and said something like, *'Little brother, let's play a game. I want you to stand in the corner until you can stop thinking about a white bear.'*

During my PhD, I spent many hours investigating whether it's possible to suppress our thoughts (of white bears and various other things). Rather than making you believe it with my words, I'd like you to give the exercise below a go:

▲ Put a timer on your phone for five minutes.
▲ Picture a romantic partner (potential or real) wearing a mankini.

▲ Press start on the timer and for the
five-minute period don't think about the
romantic partner you just pictured.

▲ If you do think about them then put a tally
mark somewhere.

▲ Write your experience of the exercise onto
that notes page of your smartphone (or the
stone/journal if you've gone old skool).

In the story, by asking his little brother to *not* think
about something, the older brother guaranteed
himself a fair amount of peace.

How did you get on? Most people tend to think
about the thing they're *not* supposed to be thinking
about many times, and in doing so they see that it's
really difficult to suppress their thoughts. In other
words, trying not to think about something that's
bothering us probably isn't the best strategy.

Do not think about this bear

Chapter 2

Exercise

Our overprotective minds

In the last chapter, I taught you that when psychological discomfort comes along, trying to avoid it won't work. You could view this newfound knowledge as the first tool I've given you, because now you know what *not* to do. However, obviously, that isn't enough. You also need to know, concretely speaking, how to move forward positively in your life. The rest of this book is going to help with that. It's going to give you a blueprint for how to improve your psychological wellbeing. And if you can improve your psychological wellbeing, then the world is your oyster.

    OK, so what I'm about to say might sound odd, but bear with me. When psychological discomfort comes along, who tells us to try to avoid it? Think back to the example where I'm about to go to a party but I'm socially phobic. The party will help me develop friendships, but it will also bring me anxiety, so I avoid the party to avoid the anxiety. Now, there's no doubt that the popularity of avoidance in society would have impacted my behaviour, but it was my own mind that delivered the information to me. In other words, my own mind, in the hope that it could convince me to avoid the party, fed me unhelpful thoughts, often in the form of images. Possibly some of these may resonate with you:

- *You'll have no one to stand next to in there.*

- *You'll probably say something embarrassing.*

- *There'll be plenty of other parties in the future.*

- *Do you remember the last party you went to? Those people laughed so hard when you dropped that drink on your toe.*

The funny thing about our minds is that we take them so seriously, and yet, deep inside we know that we probably shouldn't. Have you ever been in a situation where you were standing at the top of a building and your mind said, *'Jump!'*? Or while driving across a bridge, has your mind ever said, *'You could drive off this bridge'*? If you've been in these types of situations and yet are still reading these words, it suggests that sometimes our minds are a bit random and that sometimes it's best to not listen to them. People find it strange to think like this (at least to begin with) because it feels so natural to place confidence in our minds. But our minds are not perfect.

You see, people don't often view their minds in the same way that they view other muscles in their body, with regard to their usefulness. For example, if I ask you to get from the sofa to the door, then you'd probably use your legs to get you there because, in that context, they're the best tool for the job. You wouldn't walk on your arms because they just aren't too useful for the task at hand (excuse the pun).

It's the same with our minds: their usefulness is dependent on the context. If your dog rolls in fox poop (Dora did this morning), then your mind is the perfect problem-solving device. This morning, my mind prompted me to look for a tap to shower Dora, it prompted me to look for puddles to wash her in and it finally reminded me that there are buckets of warm water available at the park (which I ended up throwing over her with a tad too much zeal). However, if I was just about to give a presentation, attend an exam, talk to someone that I had conflict with or ask someone out on a date, my mind would be the opposite of my friend.

It's our ancestors' fault

In some ways, this quirk of the human mind makes absolute sense. Our learning experiences, across generations, influence who we are. Think back to an early ancestor of ours, the caveman. Given the difficult environment at the time, the caveman's main job was to stay alive. In other words, his mind served one primary purpose: it was a threat-detector machine. Once a threat was detected, then his mind's job was to figure out how to escape it. So, if the caveman saw a rustle in the bushes ahead, his mind probably said, *'Best steer clear of that bush'*, even if there were berries on it, because it was better to miss lunch than to *be* lunch. Is it really surprising, therefore, that our minds sometimes push us to avoid? They were bred to watch out for threats and to protect us from them.

In fact, the very reason that I'm writing, and you're reading, these words, is probably because our ancestors were good at spotting and avoiding danger (our ancestors were basically *The Croods* – pencil that film in for a Sunday afternoon in the future when you've no energy left to play *shopkeeper* or *teachers* with your gorgeous but demanding child). So, when I'm approaching that party, my mind is just doing what minds have evolved to do; it's detecting a threat (the social situation) and trying to protect me from it (by feeding me thoughts that will convince me to avoid the discomfort of the situation). However, nowadays we don't live in a world with the same sort of danger that our ancient ancestors faced, and by rigidly listening to our minds, we may find ourselves moving away from things that are important to us (social connection in the party example).

Let's get moving

In order to make positive changes in our lives then, we need to become more aware of the fact that our minds are not always good for us. And one positive change that we really need to make, where our minds can often play an obstruc-tive role, is with regard to the amount of exercise we do.

It may pain you to learn this, but exercise is supremely good for us. However, there's more nuance to it than that.

Firstly, if your body is strong then your mind will have less to worry about, and **those who exercise more tend to have**

35

stronger bodies. They have less risk of death and improved functioning with regard to immunity, the cardiovascular system, the metabolic system and weight management.

Secondly, **people who exercise tend to have better mental health** than those who don't exercise. It won't take you long to find information supporting this idea. The internet will give you various stories from people who describe the positive benefits of exercise on their psychological well-being. Even celebrities swear by exercise as a way to improve their mental health (Eminem, Lena Dunham, Harry Judd, Demi Lovato, Dacre Montgomery and Khloé Kardashian to name but a few. Yes, I do know who those people are).

Importantly, however, these stories are backed up by empirical research. Exercise can prevent mental health problems from occurring in the first place and has been shown to reduce symptoms of depression, anxiety and other psychological troubles, in people from all generations. One study found that improvements in mood could happen after only a single ten-minute session. Indeed, even those with severe depression can show marked improvement after following an exercise regime, and exercise can outperform psychotherapy and anti-depressants as treatments for depression. In younger people like you, the research broadly tells the same story. An appropriate amount of exercise per week results in better physical and psychological wellbeing. It's also related to better cognitive development, performance, learning and academic achievement, which is pretty important if you happen to be a university student.

If you want even more nuance, then participation in sports

(team sports in particular) and moderate-intense exercise has been found to be especially impactful. For those of you who don't know, moderate-intense exercise means doing something that allows you to burn three to six times more energy than you would when sitting still. Some surprising examples of this include cleaning heavily, mowing the lawn, moving household/garage items and even sex (it goes without saying that sex is the best option out of those just listed). Moderate-intense exercise is thought to affect us positively because (1) it's not too demanding and (2) it lends itself well to routine and subsequently brings structure to our weeks.

Fancy a run?

All of this means *yay* for exercise. Whether it's running, walking, cycling, cleaning, playing a sport, dancing, gardening, sex, the gym or some combination of those things, exercise makes us feel good. Given its remarkable impact, it seems prudent to get into the habit of exercise as soon as we possibly can, yes? How about right now? How about you put down this book, put on your shorts and trainers and a T-shirt and go for a fifteen-minute run? Yes or no? Take a couple of minutes to think about this.

I'm curious as to what happened in your mind in that couple of minutes. What thoughts did you have after I asked you to do this thing that's quite obviously good for you? If your mind was saying, *'Great, let's do it!'*, then you're good to go. You can load upbeat music onto your smartphone (believe it or not, Tinie Temper is my running music at the moment), get on with the act of exercising, and pick up from this sentence when you get back. (Note: by telling you that Tinie Temper is my running music I was trying to subtly let you know that I'm proper cool. It was only when a student of mine read an early version of this book that they pointed out how *Temper* is actually spelt *Tempah*. The irony, eh? Turns out I'm not so cool after all.)

Right now, you've either just returned from a good run (perhaps consider having a shower) or you're in another camp of people. And this is the camp of people I'm most interested in because the people in this camp probably had minds that weren't too helpful. My guess would be that this camp is the bigger one, because, as I wrote above, minds can often be obstructive. I'm going to guess that some of the following thoughts strolled in and out of your awareness:

- *It's raining, I'll get ill.*

- *Does he mean now? Does he really want us to do this or is he just trying to make a point?*

- *Maybe I'll read to the end of the chapter before I run.*

- *I've got a twisted ankle.*

- *I'll do it tomorrow.*

- *Nic isn't going to know if I do this.*

- *I'm on an aeroplane.*

- *I'm too embarrassed to run looking like I do.*

- *I don't have any trainers.*

- *I may get chased by a psychopathic racoon.*

Hurdling our passengers

When we start to move towards things that are important to our wellbeing, our mind will sometimes put hurdles or barriers in the way. Some of the barriers we face will be external or physical (and therefore we can't do too much about them) and some of the barriers will be internal. Have a look at the list above and see if you can spot the **physical barriers**. There are only three (twisted ankle, on an aeroplane, don't have trainers). The rest are **internal barriers**: thoughts that your mind has fed you that aren't really good reasons for not doing the exercise. And the problem with internal barriers is that they can impact our behaviour so quickly. We have the thoughts and, before we know it, we're sat on the sofa with a big bag of popcorn and a bottle of red wine while repeat episodes of *Big Bang Theory* or *Brooklyn Nine-Nine* play on the TV (I'm hoping that's not just me).

What can we do about this state of affairs? Well, we need to get better at spotting the barriers that our minds put in front of us. If we can do this then we might just have a chance at hurdling the barriers, or – to say this another way – we might just have a chance at building exercise into our lives going forward. I find one metaphor particularly good for helping me to understand the impact that my thoughts can have on my behaviour, and this metaphor has allowed me to spot unhelpful thoughts over the past few years and commit to exercising in spite of them (I'm absolutely not making this up. I've made the transition from dad-bod to decent-bod). The metaphor, which is called *Passengers on the Bus*, goes something like this.

Passengers on the bus

Imagine that you're a bus driver. You get to drive your bus wherever you like. This is much like your life: you get to move in directions that are important to you. While driving your bus of life, you see somewhere that you want to go in the distance. For argument's sake, let's call it *going for a run*. You start driving towards this special place. The problem is that as you begin to move in this direction, a number of passengers run to the front of the bus. They can be scary, aggressive, persuasive, cunning and are generally unhelpful. They try in any way they can to make you drive an alternative route. For example, one passenger might say, *'It's raining outside, you'll get ill if you run now.'* Once you do change the route, the passengers go back to their seats and leave you alone. More often than not, therefore, you'll heed the warning of the passengers, change your route, and drive aimlessly around the city. By doing this, you never really move towards that important place you want to be, and of course your mental health suffers as a consequence.

A few weeks of driving around go by and then you see the goal of *going for a run* again. You start driving towards it. The passengers run to the front of the bus and start being unhelpful. However, this time you slow down, you acknowledge your passengers, you put on your trainers and get out of the door. As you do this, you realise three things:

1. Every time we drive towards somewhere important, passengers will likely show up. Unfortunately, our mind will put up barriers on most occasions when we're about to exercise given that the process of exercise can be unpleasant.

2. There's no way to remove the passengers or to make

them stop their sneaky ways. Unwanted thoughts and feelings are like this – it's very difficult to get rid of or change them.

3. As persuasive as these passengers are, we don't have to follow their advice.

Introducing defusion

The *Passengers on the Bus* metaphor illustrates a psychological technique that I use to help me exercise, which involves slowing down the process of thinking so that I can distance myself from the thoughts that my mind has fed me, and spot when they're being unhelpful, in light of what's important to me. Read that sentence again – it's an important one. The technique is called *defusion* and there are a couple of interesting things about defusion that I want to explore briefly (I'm somewhat of a geek so when I say *interesting* – there's a chance that you won't find it as interesting as I do. Nevertheless, for you, knowing this information will help you to better understand defusion, which will help you to incorporate it into your life more easily).

Firstly, defusion involves the curious idea that our thoughts don't have to cause our behaviour. This might sound odd at first, but I can illustrate it for you. Think to yourself this thought, *'Jump up and down.'* Keep repeating that command in your head. *'Jump up and down, jump up and down, jump up and down.'* At the same time, be as still as a stone. How did you get on? Did you manage to stay still? Of course you did. But how is this possible if thoughts control what we do? If you repeat this exercise with any instruction, you'll eventually realise that we don't have to act in the way that our thoughts tell us to.

My gut says that you already know this. I bet there have been loads of times when your mind has told you to do something stupid and you've managed to not do it. This is definitely the case for me (my mind once told me to steal a cat and dress it in a funky costume but, luckily, I didn't listen to my mind on that occasion). In defusion, what we're talking about is expanding this skill of having thoughts and not acting on them. You see, when we become overly attached to our thoughts, they can impact our behaviour negatively. But what if we can get some distance from them? Would it be possible to notice our thoughts and still control our behaviour appropriately? Let me tell you that it is possible to do this. It's possible to distance yourself from the unhelpful advice of your mind, and choose your actions carefully, and I'm going to give you some techniques to help with this later on.

But before that, let's talk about the other curious thing to know about defusion. There are some thoughts that are particularly tricky to manage, and those are thoughts that could turn out to be true, or thoughts that have some truth to them. But being defused involves letting go of *truth*. It instead involves evaluating thoughts based only on their usefulness in relation to what's important to us, not whether they're true or not. In other words, whenever we encounter some advice from our mind, we ask ourselves this question, *'Would acting on this thought help me move towards the important thing I want to move towards?'*

As an example, imagine the thought, *'Someone in the university gym will laugh at me if I use a running machine because of my silly running style, so I'd better not do that.'* There's a chance that thought might be true. I may indeed have a silly running style and someone from the university gym may indeed laugh at me. However, when living in the world of defusion, I don't care about truth. I focus on usefulness in light of what I want. In other words, would taking that thought seriously move me towards this important wellbeing activity? Probably not.

In some ways, defusion simply involves changing the way we respond to our thoughts. Just like the *Passengers on the Bus* metaphor, we learn to distance ourselves from our thoughts and evaluate them based on whether they're useful in helping us to pursue the life we want to be living. If they're useful, then we follow their advice; if they're not useful, then we thank our mind for its efforts and focus our energy on what we want to be doing at that point in time. We learn to treat thoughts as just thoughts, bits of language in our head that might or might not be useful.

A simple but powerful defusion exercise, that you could practise most days easily enough, involves adding the prefix *'I'm having the thought that'* to the thoughts that push us around. This prefix creates a little more space between our thoughts and us, such that we become freer to choose our actions. For example, imagine that after I asked you to engage in some exercise you thought, *'I'll go for a run later instead of right now.'* If you used the prefix, it would have become, *'I'm having the thought that I'll go for a run later instead of right now.'* Did you notice the subtle shift? Something felt different when using the prefix. This is because using the prefix reminds us how minds work (that they can sometimes be unhelpful), it gives us a little distance from our thoughts, and it therefore helps us to make better choices. By being more aware of my own thoughts, by distancing myself from them and by analysing their usefulness on the basis of my goals, I've managed to build exercise into my life (rather than being pushed around by the silly thoughts that my mind sometimes feeds me).

The take-home

OK, that was quite a lot of psychobabble, but I hope that some of it made sense. Exercise is really important. Human beings always forget that psychological suffering doesn't happen in a vacuum. The research is clear on this. If we don't take care of our sleep, if we don't eat well and if we don't exercise then our psychological wellbeing will get worse. Most of us already know this and yet still live relatively unhealthy lives.

The reason for this contradiction is that our minds sometimes stop us from doing activities when they're difficult. Imagine you're about to go to the gym. How often has your mind interjected with *'I'm too tired'* or *'I'll do it tomorrow instead'?* It's not that minds are bad or faulty (they evolved to be this way), it's just that they're usually quick to come up with reasons for not doing things, even when those things are important. Knowing this makes the job of managing our sometimes unhelpful minds more do-able. We don't have to become angry with or try to change our minds or the thoughts they feed us, we just have to become more aware of why they occur and how they influence our decision-making.

Some of you may love exercise and do plenty of it already. However, there'll be many others, reading this chapter while devouring a large slab of chocolate cake, who may well have a persistent motivation problem. In other words, when they think about exercise, their minds feed them thoughts that don't, in any way, make them pumped for exercise.

The thing about motivating thoughts is that often we have to wait a long time for them to come along. But what if we didn't need motivation in order to exercise? What if we could exercise in the absence of motivating thoughts? Wouldn't that be cool? Well, defusion can help with this. It involves becoming more aware of our thoughts, spotting when they're being unhelpful, and controlling our behaviour accordingly. If, in crucial moments when we lack the motivation to exercise, we can learn to better relate to our thoughts, then we'll be able to do exercise even when our minds are being the awkward little buttercups they can be.

Chapter 2 Tasks

Task 1 – Practising defusion

Defusion is all about getting better at noticing our thoughts, and a great way to improve our defusion skill is via a three-minute meditation exercise that asks you to put your thoughts on the slides of a PowerPoint presentation and simply watch them (sounds strange but give it a go). Below are some instructions for how to do this. Read them before you begin the exercise:

▲ Visualise being sat in a lecture theatre.

▲ Thoughts pop in and out of your mind while you're there, and they appear on the slides of the PowerPoint presentation on the big screen in front of you.

▲ Each slide will represent your thoughts in words or pictures.

▲ A slide may hang around for a little bit, or it may pop off the screen quickly. That's fine. If a slide hangs around, then continue to watch it. If it leaves the screen, then watch it leave.

▲ If your mind seems to stop giving you thoughts, then keep watching the screen because they'll come back.

▲ If your mind says, *'I'm rubbish at this'* or *'This is*

a silly exercise', then watch those thoughts on
the big screen too.

▲ Set a timer for three minutes on your smartphone, close your eyes and begin the exercise.

The idea with this task is to get better at slowing
down and noticing our thoughts. If we can do that
then we'll be in a better place to listen to, or not
listen to, the advice they give us. Record your experience of the exercise on the notes page of your
smartphone. Here are some things you might like to
write about:

- Was it weird to watch your thoughts?

- Did the exercise create some distance
  between you and them?

- When you're just about to do exercise and
  your mind is being obstructive, would a bit of
  defusion help you to better achieve your goals?

- When you've started exercise but your mind
  feeds you self-deprecating thoughts (mine
  sometimes says, *'Your face is so red that
  other people will worry your head is going
  to explode'*), then would a bit of defusion help
  you to continue with the exercise?

- Outside of exercise, could having the ability
  to watch your thoughts be useful to you in the
  real world?

Task 2 – Building exercise into our lives

OK, if we're going to get into the habit of exercising then we need a plan, and this plan needs to take into account how minds work. Follow my instructions below and write some answers on the notes page of your smartphone. I'm going to do this too and I'll write my answers below for you to see:

On which days will you exercise?

Monday, Wednesday and Friday.

What types of exercising are available for you to do on these days?

Walking, running, playing football, lifting weights, bodyweight exercises, squash.

Note: there's plenty of variety in how we can exercise, and what's wonderful is that we get to choose the type of exercise we do. What am I saying here? Although exercising can often be unpleasant, and although we now have defusion to help us navigate our way through such unpleasant experiences, if you can choose enjoyable exercise activities then you'll have fewer passengers on your bus to deal with. So be pragmatic, if you hate running but quite like yoga, then choose yoga.

What internal barriers (thoughts and feelings) are likely to visit you on the days you plan to exercise?

- I can't be bothered.
- It's been a long day.
- I'll do it tomorrow.
- I don't really care about this.
- It's more important that I spend time with my wife and my boy.
- Writing this book is essential, exercising isn't.

When those thoughts come along, what can you do with them?

I can defuse them. I can use the 'I'm having the thought' prefix. I can also picture thoughts as passengers on my bus, whereby I know I can have them and yet still drive to where I want to go.

How long do you plan to complete this routine for?

Six weeks. After which I'll reassess how I exercise and will endeavour to write a new plan.

How will you feel if you complete this plan?

I'll feel good that I managed to exercise more, and I'll feel good that I'm using the skill of defusion to help me do this. However, I want to see if exercising is having any impact on my wellbeing too, so I plan to monitor how I feel after each training session. I'll also take weight measurements and pictures of my body to note any changes. It will be interesting to see how these things fluctuate across time.

If you fail at the plan (e.g., miss a session or more), then what will you do?

This is an ongoing thing. There'll be times when my mind gets the better of me, and that's fine as minds are powerful devices that have evolved to reduce discomfort. But if I do miss a session, or fall off the wagon, then I'll revert to the plan as quickly as possible and try not to beat myself up too much about it.

Chapter 3

Challenge Yourself

Swinging for the stars

I've just finished watching a brilliant TV programme about the flamboyant and controversial boxer Tyson Fury (look him up if you've yet to come across him). For someone like me, who's interested in wellbeing, there was a lot to take from this programme. For example:

- In the introduction we talked about how mental health problems are so common that we're normal, rather than abnormal, if we experience them. The TV programme illustrated this point nicely by showing how a man, who from the outside had everything, came within a whisker of committing suicide.

- We've also talked about how people tend to resort to unhelpful avoidance behaviours to manage unwanted thoughts and feelings. The programme showed how Tyson Fury used alcohol, drugs and food to try to make himself feel a little less rotten. I did have the guilty thought that I'd have liked to have been there for some of the partying in this period as it looked fun, but the psychologist in me could see how destructive these coping behaviours were.

- Finally, we've explored how exercise is such an important wellbeing behaviour for human beings. The programme illustrated this by showing the relationship between gym time and mental health in the life of Tyson Fury. At one point, I believe, the boxer said something like, *'I'm in the gym every day except for Sunday, which is the worst day of my week.'*

One other thing jumped out at me, which is particularly interesting in the context of this chapter. Tyson Fury became the heavyweight champion of the world in 2015 and spiralled out of control shortly afterwards. Temporally speaking, he had a challenge, the challenge ended, and then he went downhill. During the documentary, his family pointed to this issue by saying that when he was training for a fight, there was nothing to worry about, but after a fight had ended, they needed to keep an eye on him. What am I getting at here? When Tyson Fury was chasing something, or challenging himself, Tyson Fury flourished.

The benefits of challenge

Research on this topic tells the same story about the human race writ large. People who are psychologically healthy tend to be those who continue to challenge themselves in some way or another. The obvious challenge that you're undertaking right now is academic learning, and the great thing for you about this particular challenge is that it tends to be related to better wellbeing. For example, the amount of time spent studying is predictive of better mental health, and people who keep learning tend to do better on a bunch of other things too: cognitive skills, confidence, resilience, civic engagement, life satisfaction and even health behaviours (one study found that increased participation in learning courses actually made a difference to smoking cessation and exercise efforts).

Outside of education, however, there are a number of other potential challenges that could bring a different sort of vitality to your life (rather than the learning associated with your university degree – which, if we're being honest, may feel a bit of a slog a lot of the time). These challenges could take many different forms, and they could be big or small. A new exercise goal (like the one that you created in the last chapter), perhaps, or learning to play an instrument or learning a new language. How about developing car-fixing skills, plumbing skills or woodwork skills – learning to paint, learning to cook a certain cuisine, learning about the ancient Greek philosophers or learning about the intricacies of Kama Sutra (sorry, Grandma). It doesn't really matter what it is that you're trying to achieve, just that you're trying to achieve something (and luckily for us human beings there are plenty of ways to keep busy these days).

In this chapter, I want you to start thinking about some

challenges that might interest you, and what concrete things you can do to bring those challenges to life. So pull up that notes page on your smartphone and write down some things that you'd like to try to get better at. I don't think it will take you long to do this because I'm convinced that, deep inside, we each have a *that's what I'd get better at if I had the time* list. I can tell you what's on my list with no effort. I'd love to be able to play the guitar, I'd love to be able to speak French fluently and I'd love to improve my dancing skills (that last one might catch you by surprise but I've reached a point in my life where the *two-step* is no longer enough).

OK, I'm going to assume that you've spent a couple of minutes making that list. Now all you have to do is choose a challenge (I'm going to choose dancing), begin it and, in time, complete it. *'Lol!'* you might be thinking, knowing too well that life isn't that simple.

I wish we would hear a piece of advice like *challenge yourself* and then just get on with the challenge until it's done. But often that doesn't happen. Why? Because of something we've already talked about, the mind's obstructive tendencies. We've looked at how stepping back from our unhelpful thoughts may be useful in encouraging us to exercise, and there's no doubt that defusion could also be useful to us when it comes to challenge. However, now I want to add to your arsenal of psychological know-how by spending some time exploring *self-stories* and how, if we let them, they can stop us from taking on and completing challenges.

Looking into your self

So what is a self-story? Our minds have this incredible ability to draw upon past experiences (*The last time I tried to learn to dance, I failed miserably*) and then use those experiences to build stories about who we *really* are (*I'm just not a dance type person, I don't have that sort of brain, so best to get on with something else*). In case you were wondering, I didn't make up that example. When I was seventeen years old, I took my school shoes to a tap dance class that was filled with middle-aged women, who promptly danced the socks off me. The self-story that I'm not a good dancer has followed me around ever since. In fact, even these days, my only criterion for choosing a bar on a night out is that the dance-floor area is dark, so that no one else can see my rhythmless body moving around.

These self-stories creep into our lives without being noticed but they're actually pretty easy to spot because they usually show themselves with two little words: *'I am'*. These words are used at the beginning of sentences that have the purpose of describing who we are (whether referring to our personalities or our abilities). Some examples might include:

- *I am kind*
- *I am helpful*
- *I am helpless*
- *I am anxious*
- *I am confident*

- *I am a good public speaker*
- *I am broken*
- *I am honest*
- *I am humble*
- *I am creative*
- *I am boring*
- *I am geeky*
- *I am positive*
- *I am smart*
- *I am stupid*

Now some of these self-stories can be good for us. For example, if I have an *I am kind* self-story then it's likely that I'll be kind should the opportunity arise for me to show kindness. I'd be living by my story. However, the problem with many of these *I am* stories is that often they don't help us to function well at all. I want to tell you about a couple of experiences I had as a young man to illustrate the impact that unhelpful self-stories can have when we move towards challenges. My hope is that reading about these will help you to better spot your own self-stories. If you can manage this, you'll be capable of having a go at absolutely any challenge.

I should have been a footballer

I love football. It makes sense: my dad was football obsessed and my brother and I grew up with a ball at our feet. My brother Danny was always so naturally good. With a sweet left foot, he was thought of as the *sporty one* and I – with a lack of ability – was thought of as the *academic one*. It's funny – some people still hold onto those stories to this day in ways that might have impacted us both. Anyhow, suffice to say that I wasn't very good (for example, my own dad regularly benched me for the local football team that he coached ... I still hold that against him). I bought into the stories to a certain degree also but, at the time, I had something that protected me. I had the attitude that if I practised I could get better. And so, I practised and practised and practised. Soon I was one of the best players in the local league and, shortly afterwards, this old lecturer was offered a trial at a professional football club. All well and good up to this point.

I still remember getting to the stadium for the first time. It was late one evening and the pitch looked glorious (bearing in mind that I grew up playing football on tennis courts or boggy parks). I knew that I wanted to be out there in front of thousands of people. I won't bore you with too many details, but I had some great times during my trial period. However, the six months also had its fair share of negatives:

1. **It was socially awkward.** The football club was deciding which of its youngsters to offer a contract and many of the boys playing for the under 16s side had known each other for years. That is, if I was offered a contract, then someone else was dumped. So I was a threat. I didn't make any friends during my time there despite considering myself to be a nice lad.

In fact, I was isolated. All of the boys lived in a shared house while I lived alone in a local bed and breakfast.

2. **I missed my family.** Every time I left them at the train station, I shed tears on that four-hour journey. I would have done anything to get back from training and just sit with them for a while, rather than having to kill twenty hours by myself in the B&B.

3. **I didn't enjoy football when it was broken down into regimented drills.** And probably more importantly, I wasn't very good at football in that format.

4. **My legs seemed to be failing me.** I pulled muscles really easily. This meant that I spent more time not doing the one thing I loved doing and it meant more time having to deal with the ambiguities of the situation (would I be offered a contract or not?).

I took matters into my own hands. Due to these negative experiences I knew that I wasn't built to be a footballer. This challenge was too much for someone like me. Someone who wasn't *likeable,* someone who wasn't *independent* or *resilient,* and someone who wasn't *good enough* or *physically strong enough* to play the game well. I rang the youth secretary of the football club and told him that professional football wasn't for me. After a long conversation, he told me that he wouldn't be able to get me home, as he was out of the country. I told him not to worry. I caught a bus to the local train station, bought a ticket (was nearly robbed of my bag by two men on the train), got off at a central UK train station, waited for two hours, got on a new train and arrived home around 2 a.m. My mum and dad picked me up and the total relief I felt at seeing them is still hard to describe. At 7 a.m. that same morning, I arrived at my school to pick up some important exam results. I got straight As, and I broke down in the head teacher's office. It felt like I'd made the correct decision – I was the *academic type* after all.

As time went on, I continued to convince myself that I'd done the right thing. I had to, because acknowledging anything other than that would have allowed regret to trickle into my life (and nobody likes regret). But as I've grown older and wiser the following statements have become stuck in my head: *I'm not built to be a footballer, I'm not likeable, I'm not independent or resilient, I'm not good enough or physically strong enough to play the game well* and *I'm the academic type.*

When I was younger, I challenged myself to become a professional footballer. Football was a pure and beautiful thing that I wanted to do for the rest of my life. Unfortunately, however, reflecting on my experiences, I've come to the conclusion that my mind sold me a bunch of unhelpful self-stories. And I bought them. And I used them to inform my decision to quit this challenge. My mind had convinced me that all those self-stories were true and fixed parts of my make-up, and I allowed them to stop me chasing a dream.

Fast forward a few months. I was no longer playing football and I'd started a new challenge, college. Unfortunately, however, the As that I'd received in secondary school had turned into Cs at college. After a couple of years, and many a re-sit, I needed two As and a B to be accepted into my top university choice. I knew I'd be getting an A in French due to an exquisitely written piece of coursework about Eric Cantona (a brilliant French footballer), and I knew that I could get a B at politics. What I needed to do was to get an A in my favourite subject, psychology. I studied harder than I ever had by writing thirty essays and learning them by heart in preparation for the exam. But it wasn't good enough. I didn't get the A and I couldn't get into the university that I wanted to attend. Shortly after receiving the results, I decided that *I wasn't smart enough* to go to university, and so I made other plans for my future. History was repeating itself. When I was sixteen years old self-stories stopped me from trying to become a professional footballer, and a couple of years later, self-stories were going to stop me from enrolling in university.

Fast forward to Thursday 1 June, 2017. That lad with an *I'm not smart enough* self-story is now a thirty-three-year-old man with a psychology degree and a PhD (i.e., people address me as *Dr*, which is pretty stupendous). He's written a book about academic research, conducted a number of scientific studies and has just co-published an article in the *New Scientist* magazine. This article is one of the biggest impact writings about Relational Frame Theory (which is a theory of language). That is, more people probably laid their eyes on that article than for any other Relational Frame Theory article that existed at the time. On the evening the article was published, that thirty-three-year-old man sat down with a beer and basked in what felt like a big deal. It felt like an *I made it* moment. And, of course, that *I made it* moment existed in the context of his history, in the context of the many moments where him *making it* was impossible because of his *I'm not smart enough* self-story.

The turning point

How did I do it? What happened when I was eighteen years old that stopped history from repeating itself? Well, I came across Acceptance and Commitment Therapy (ACT), and the work of Dr Louise McHugh in particular. Broadly speaking, the aim of ACT is to help people develop what's called psychological flexibility. It sounds complex but it isn't. Psychological flexibility means developing the skills to experience all thoughts and feelings, positive and negative, while still moving one's feet in valued directions.

One aspect of the ACT model that I found particularly appealing was called *The Conceptualised Self*, which refers to that fact that we human beings easily build stories about who we *really* are, and that if we believe those stories strongly enough then they can create a prison for us. When I read about the conceptualised self, everything became clear for me. At sixteen years old, my self-stories convinced me to avoid the challenge of professional football (*I'm not built to be a footballer*). At college, my self-stories were trying to convince me not to go to university (*I'm not smart enough to go to university*). In both instances, the self that I'd conceptualised (sometimes called *self-as-story*), a self that I assumed was true and fixed, was impacting my ability to take on challenges. I had to do something quickly. I accepted a place at another university and the rest, as they say, is history.

Prisoner of your stories

Exploring self-stories

Given how self-stories can be so harmful in our lives, I guess you might be wondering why we have them. The truth is that they can be quite useful. Specifically, they're like cognitive short cuts: they give us easy-to-access information for how to behave in the situations we find ourselves in.

Said another way, we love to put other people into little boxes in our mind, and when we do, the world becomes a more straightforward place to live in. For example, imagine we build some stories about two of our university classmates. Let's say that *Mei is kind* and *Mo is rude*. By putting Mei and Mo into little boxes (metaphorically speaking, of course), decision-making becomes easier. For example, if there's a seat available next to Mei or Mo in a seminar room, then I know who to sit next to.

We also like to put ourselves into little boxes, and when we do, decision-making again becomes easier. For example, if you have the self-story, *I'm not a confident person*, then you know not to ask a question during a lecture because that's beyond what your personality will allow. But wow! Is that the world you want to live in? Where you don't get to do stuff because of a self-story?

In addition to wondering why self-stories develop, you might also be wondering why they have so much power over us. It's for two reasons.

1. Many of our self-stories don't actually originate with the words *'I am'* – they start with the words *'You are'*. As we grow up, the people who we trust (e.g.,

parents/teachers) will tell us who we truly are and it makes sense to believe them, because to deny the self-story would be to deny the people who gave it to us.

2. Many self-stories that we have are built from our personal experiences and therefore they feel *real* or *true*. Let me give you an example of this. I remember being a sixteen-year-old boy asking a sixteen-year-old girl out on a date. She said *'No'*. Apparently, my poems just didn't do it for her (no joke, I still love the odd bit of poetry). Anyhow, my friends said that I didn't look confident when I approached her, and I certainly didn't feel confident. For a couple of years following the event, every time there was an opportunity to interact with a girl, I avoided it, because I just wasn't the *confident type*. Here, one real experience stuck with me, became a self-story and impacted my subsequent behaviour.

And this is pretty much the norm. We tend to look at these *I am* stories as if they represent truth because they're based on our experiences, and therefore we assume that they have the right both to define who we are and to influence our behaviour. There are two things that I want to say about this.

One: should we trust the accuracy of our self-stories?

Do you trust your own mind to give you accurate information about your own experiences? Let's play a memory game. Can you remember what happened on your sixth birthday? What was the order of the day? Who was present? What toys did you get? How about four days after your sixth birthday? Can you remember what happened on that day? What did you have for breakfast? What day of the week was it? How about twenty-seven days after your sixth birthday? What clothes were you wearing? What lessons did you have in school? Which friends did you play with?

I bet you have no memory of any of those days and yet they were filled with experiences that could confirm or disconfirm your self-stories. So, who chooses what we get to remember and what we get to forget? And does this happen in an objective sort of way? No, it doesn't. What actually happens is that we look for and remember information from our lives that supports what we already think to be *true* about ourselves (it's called a confirmation bias). In fact, chances are that we've all met people who have changed actual historical events in their minds, and believe them, simply because it allows them to confirm stuff about themselves and others.

With these things in mind, if you could go back and watch your life like you would watch a movie, I bet you'd find a big gap between who you think you truly are and the experiences you've actually had. For example, if you believe you're an honest person, I bet there have been a hundred times when you've lied. If you believe that you're a kind person, I bet there have been a hundred times when you've been unkind. If you believe you're a hardworking person, I bet there have been a hundred times when you've been lazy. Our personality characteristics – with which we interact as being stable across time and context – are often not even based on what's actually happened in our lives, and for that reason alone we should hold our self-stories lightly. The *reality* on which we base our decisions is built on sand.

To be clearer, although self-stories are built from our experiences, they're not built from *all* of our experiences. This leads me to a place where I now don't trust the stories that my own mind feeds me about myself, and definitely not enough to use them when making important decisions. There are a couple of very interesting consequences of taking this position.

1. It means that I pay little attention to other people's opinions about me. We live in a world, especially with the advances made in social media, where other people will have built stories about you in their own mind and will be more than happy to tell you who *you* are. Well, fuck them. Because if you shouldn't trust your own mind when it gives you self-stories, then you definitely shouldn't trust the views of people that have been psychologically present far less in your history than you have.

2. It also means that I give very little weight to my own

opinions about other people. Why? Because if other people can't remember twenty-seven days after their own sixth birthday, then I sure as hell can't. I've been around for a lot less of their life than they have and so what right do I have to make sweeping generalisations about them?

Two: should we let our self-stories influence us?

If we had a magic mirror which confirmed that all our self-stories were true and fixed parts of us, then should that stop us from doing stuff? A student of mine once told me that they couldn't come to class because *depression* was a part of their personality. A colleague of mine once turned down an interview because they weren't *good at interviews*. A friend of mine decided not to have a child because they weren't *responsible enough* to be a parent.

Imagine that all those stories were *true* in an objective sense – should we still let them create a prison for us? Because if we believe personalities and abilities to be fixed, then we have no choice in our actions – we act the way we do because that's how we're programmed. We don't get to try to attend class, be good at interviews or be a parent. In other words, we're stuck. Nothing can ever change for us. Let me tell you that living in that space, where we can't take on challenges of our choosing because of a self-story, isn't good for psychological wellbeing.

Spotting your stories

The big question, then, is this: what can we do to lessen the impact that self-stories have on our behaviour? Well, we need to get better at spotting them. And it just so happens that I've the perfect exercise to help you break into this habit, which involves improving our ability to distinguish between evaluation and description:

▲ Suppose I'm holding a mobile telephone, and I describe it in the following way, *'My mobile phone has a black screen, is slightly smaller than my hand and has a camera facility.'*

▲ Upon seeing my mobile phone, you would be able to agree with that sentence from an objective position.

▲ But imagine I then added to the description the following words, *'My mobile phone is the best mobile phone in the world.'*

▲ At this point you might step in with an objection on the basis that the second sentence isn't a description, it's an evaluation.

Now let me apply this logic to a human being (myself). There's something very different about saying, *'I am 181cm tall'* versus *'I'll never be good at dancing.'* One of those is an objective self-description and the other is a self-evaluation (or a self-story).

Many of us don't understand the difference between self-description and self-evaluation, and therefore pay them equal respect when making decisions. But if we can get better at distinguishing between them then it will help us to spot our self-stories and hold them lightly when choosing our behaviour. To give you some practice with this, pull up the notes page on your smartphone and write down ten things about yourself that begin with the words *'I am'*, and then see if you can spot the statements that are self-description versus those that are self-evaluation. You'll be surprised by how many self-evaluation statements you have. In fact, I'd predict that most of them would be in that category.

At university, there are a number of situations where having the ability to spot self-stories will come in handy, but there are two that feel particularly important to discuss:

1. Before you begin university, you may have had some unfortunate experiences (in secondary school possibly) that have led you to view yourself in a particular way. For example, you could have the self-story, *'I'm not a popular/sociable/likeable type of person.'* And then you get to university and the first social experience for you to navigate your way through is *Freshers Week*, which has the capacity to be overwhelming. In this situation, if you can spot your self-story, then you've a better chance of throwing yourself into Freshers Week.

2. Towards the end of university, you'll have to apply for jobs (or you could just prolong being a student like I did). I wonder what self-stories you might have

71

at that point, and how they might impact what jobs you go for. This sort of thing may go through your mind, *'I'm not creative enough/smart enough/ hard-working enough for that job.'* In this situation, if you can spot your self-story, then you've a better chance of applying for a job that you'd quite like.

By improving our ability to spot self-stories, we give ourselves the luxury of choice. We can choose to take them seriously, or we can choose to take them with a pinch of salt. We can choose to act on them, or we can choose to view the self-story as just that, a story. Importantly, as with our general thoughts, instead of looking at these self-stories in terms of how literally true they appear, we need to look at them in terms of how helpful they are in moving us towards what's important.

Losing our selves

As you begin to chip away at your self-stories, you may begin to worry about what sort of self you'll have left. It's a legitimate concern because detaching ourselves from our self-stories may make us feel like we're *losing our self.* For example, if I'm not who my mind tells me I am, then who am I? The answer to this question is something quite profound that can take some getting used to. What's left is the you that sees and observes the world. This *observer self* simply watches self-stories rather than being caught up in them. It's that sense of self that holds or contains all our experiences, a stable and ongoing sense of 'I' that exists independently of the self-stories our minds might feed us.

There's every chance that those last five lines make absolutely no sense to you right now, but if you're struggling to understand what the observer self is (maybe even having an *I'm not smart enough* moment), then don't worry, it's not you. The observer self isn't an idea that can be easily explained or understood verbally. In fact, it's not an idea at all, it's an experience you need to contact in order to understand it. It's a bit like the taste of an apple – no matter how many words I use, I can never explain to you what the taste is actually like. Sure, words can get us close, but a description of an event is not the event itself. The map is not the land. With this in mind, I'm hoping that the combination of a metaphor and an exercise will give you more clarity about the observer self.

Let's start with the metaphor, which compares the relationship between the observer self and our self-stories with the relationship between the sky and the weather.

We're like the sky. Our self-stories are like the weather. The weather changes constantly. Sometimes there's sunshine and sometimes there are clouds, rain or storms. Our self-stories are like this. Sometimes they're positive and sometimes they're self-defeating, restricting and negative.

There are a couple of important things to know about the relationship between the sky and the weather. Firstly, the weather can never hurt the sky in the same way that our self-stories can never hurt us. They're stories, and only that. Secondly, the sky can always hold the weather no matter how bad it is. We're the same. We can always make room for tricky self-stories no matter how powerful they seem. We often forget that the sky is there (perhaps sometimes it's hard to see the sky through the weather). When this happens, it's easy to believe that the weather and the sky are one and the same – or it's easy to believe that we are our self-stories.

However, every now and then we notice the sky: stable, broad, limitless and pure. The observer self involves learning to access the sky more, and seeing it as a place where we can make room for and watch our self-stories, rather than be defined by them.

A good way for you to access your observer self is to engage in a brief meditation-type exercise that requires you to notice who's doing the noticing. This can feel like a strange exercise, but give it a go and you may just experience something remarkable.

- ▲ Begin by closing your eyes.
- ▲ Then, for thirty seconds, simply listen to what your mind has to say. The thoughts may be positive or negative, they may be colourful or dull, they may be pictures or words and they may even stop for a while. Your job for this thirty-second period is simply to watch what happens.
- ▲ Once you've completed the exercise, record your thoughts on the notes page of your smartphone.

What did you notice? Most people will report mind

wandering, as they might do in any typical meditation exercise. However, I want you to notice something else. Specifically, I want you to notice that the exercise involved two selves. The first – let's call it your *thinking self* – provided you with your thoughts and feelings. Sometimes, it can seem as though we only have a thinking self. But who was watching and hearing the chatter of the thinking self? Who was observing? This was your second sense of self. Your *observer self* was there too.

Keeping it real

My hope is that reading this chapter has triggered a *Eureka!* moment for you, as you begin to realise the impact that self-stories have had on your life. However, it's important to be clear about something. The information I've given you isn't magic. Yes, developing the ability to spot our self-stories and hold them lightly will lessen their hold over us, but as much as we'd like to, we can't make them disappear. We have to take them with us. Indeed, some of our self-stories may even exist for the rest of our lives.

As an example, my *I'm not smart enough* story continues to follow me around despite my successes. But it doesn't stop me from taking on challenges. Funnily enough, this book is evidence of that. The second I was asked to write it, and every single day since, that self-story pops in to say *'Hello'*. But here I am, taking on this monumental challenge while my self-story sits in the room with me. Your life, like mine, is going to be filled with the opportunity to challenge yourself. No doubt, before and during your challenges you'll also find yourself saying *'Hello'* to your own unhelpful self-stories, but with a bit of luck the advice given here will enable you to keep going even when the heaviest of them is weighing you down.

The take-home

We often use the words *I am* to describe stories about ourselves. However, do these self-stories help us to live meaningful lives or do they get in the way? Do we begin to live by these stories in a way that moves us away from what we'd like to do? Do we start to use them as excuses for our behaviour? Do they imprison us? Often, self-stories can stop us from taking on and pursuing challenges, but imagine the liberation if we managed to stop them from pushing us around. Maybe, instead of following an *I am* statement with a plethora of unhelpful verbal diarrhoea that drowns us (great visual there), we could simply use the words *I am* to describe our existence. Maybe *I exist* is enough.

If we start to think about our personalities and abilities in this way, then all challenges become possible. This goes for big challenges (big-life-decision type challenges, the kind I've described in this chapter) and for smaller challenges too (hobby-type challenges, which are equally important). The principle is the same for every challenge we decide to take on where a self-story gets involved, irrespective of size. It's all about interacting with our sense of self in a more flexible way.

How do we do this? Just being aware that self-stories are a thing will help. Every time you hear the words *'I am'* (or *'I can't'*) in that mind of yours you'll know (1) to be cautious of how much you believe the self-story and (2) to look out for how the self-story influences your behaviour. It will also help to remember the *Sky and the Weather* metaphor, to remember the *observer self* that was watching your thoughts in the meditation exercise, and to remember to continue to ask yourself if your *'I am'* statements are self-description or self-evaluation.

Dr Steven C. Hayes (the main ACT fella) once coined a cool phrase, *'Kill your self everyday'*. He didn't mean literally to kill yourself (in fact, it would be remarkable if someone could repeatedly kill themselves). He meant that we should kill the impact that self-stories can have on our lives. If we hold them more lightly, we become liberated. So, let me ask you this question, *'How willing are you to let go of your self-stories in order to pursue important challenges?'*

Chapter 3 Tasks

Task 1 – Taking a look at some of your self-stories

I want you to see that you already have many stories about yourself, so follow these steps:

▲ Find a mirror and look at yourself in it (this might be an awkward experience to begin with).

▲ Start audio recording yourself and aim to make the exercise last for two to three minutes (a lot of people hate the sound of their own voice, but give yourself a break this time).

▲ Tell the mirror version of you about your self. Tell them who you are when it comes to relationships, when it comes to relaxation, when it comes to work, when it comes to spirituality, when it comes to adversity, when it comes to learning, etc.

▲ Afterwards, listen to the stories you have about yourself.

▲ Have a think about which ones are useful versus which ones hold you back. Think about how these stories have impacted, or might impact, your behaviour.

▲ Write down your experience of completing this exercise on the notes page of your smart-phone, and also write down your thoughts about what we've talked about in this chapter more broadly.

▲ Finally, write down the strongest story you have about yourself. If I were to do that then I'd have these words on my notes page, *'I'm not smart enough.'*

If you do these things then you'll be more aware of the self-stories that hold you back, and be reminded of them. Then, when those stories show themselves, you can see them exactly for what they are, stories that are not you, stories that exist independent of you, and stories that don't have to stop you from chasing challenges.

Task 2 – Let's choose a challenge and go for it

Earlier on you chose a challenge that you'd like to pursue (mine was to get better at dancing). Now we need to set about creating a goal-based action plan to get moving with that challenge. But before we do that, a little bit of advice. The best goals are precise. The more precise the goal, the easier it is to hold ourselves accountable. I'll try to model this idea in the exercise below, which I'd like you to complete on that notes page:

What's the challenge?

To become a better dancer.

How are you going to do this?

In the short term, I'd like to master some cool footwork. I aim to have five footwork dances learned in the next five months that I'll find on YouTube.

When are you going to work on this challenge?

On a Monday, Wednesday and Friday morning, for fifteen minutes each time. Probably just before I complete my exercise goal from the last chapter.

What self-stories are likely to show themselves when you do this?

That I just don't have the inbuilt coordination skills to ever be a good dancer. I'll probably also feel embarrassed, as I have a self-story about being an introvert too.

What will you do with the self-stories when they say 'Hello'?

Put them in my pocket and carry them with me as I practise.

How will you measure success in your challenge?

I'll make videos. This will allow me to see if I'm getting better. However, just keeping practising in the face of self-stories could also count as success.

How do you think you'll feel if you manage to meet this challenge?

I'll feel good that I did something positive despite a strongly held self-story, and it will inspire me to take on other challenges too, and to hold other self-stories lightly as well. Also, I'll feel great at weddings when I rip up the dance floor.

What will you do if you miss a day (or more) of the plan, or if you don't continue with this commitment?

I'll engage in a serious amount of self-loathing which will eventually allow me to confirm that my self-story was true (I'm joking). Failure is a part of the journey. I can drop the baton sometimes and still pick up the challenge at the next available opportunity.

Chapter 4

Connect with People

Persuading you to be social

Life is all about relationships with people. In fact, research shows that having good social relationships is *the best* predictor of wellbeing in people of every age category. Feelings of worth, love, intimacy, support, meaning and purpose are all higher in those who have high-quality social relationships (it's also linked to better health behaviours and living a longer life). Unfortunately, those without good social relationships are much more likely to develop mental health problems (just look at the crushing impact of separation caused by Covid-19 for evidence of this). Given the central role that connecting with other human beings has on our psychological wellbeing, I'm going to spend a couple of chapters exploring human relationships. I'll also equip you with some skills for navigating your way through what can be a tricky social environment.

Connecting

I'm going to start in what might seem like an odd place. Around 2014, I began teaching an area of psychology that I knew very little about. This happens more than you might imagine in academia. Researchers with absolutely no experience of *Intelligence*, *Memory* or *Abnormal Psychology* are required to teach those exact subjects to a class full of students. It's rather intimidating. And it's made even more intimidating by the fact that you university students can be like hawks hunting for prey. My experience is that some of the more unscrupulous students are on the lookout for lecturers who don't know what they're talking about because they can then use the lecturer's incompetence as an excuse for poor marks later in the term. I know this because I used to be one of those students. The number of times I would say to my mum, *'OK, so I got a 48, but the lecturer on that module was rubbish.'*

Knowing that such a group of untoward characters awaited my new module on the *Psychology of Influence*, I decided I should become an expert on the subject matter, therefore putting myself in a position to avoid that awkward moment where some smart-arse student points out an inconsistency in my teaching. The topic seemed interesting enough, but I had no idea where to begin my study. It turned out that only one resource was needed to teach this course, a book written by social psychologist Dr Robert Cialdini, which essentially answered this question, *'How do I influence people'?*

'Hang on,' I hear you say. What on Earth has the psychology of influence got to do with wellbeing or connecting

with others? Well, there are a variety of people in our environments with whom we build relationships. Many of those people are not close to us, but are important, none-theless. Why? Because we need things from them in order to prosper. I'm thinking of bosses, colleagues, neighbours, clients, friends and even university lecturers. The rationale goes like this: people who are good at persuading others also tend to be successful, and people who are successful improve their chances of psychological wellbeing. In other words, learning how to persuade people will help you to better operate in your wider social world. So, let me tell you about the six magical principles that Cialdini put together.

Commitment – 'But I promised'

There's a story I want to tell you, concerning a problem that toy stores had and how they solved it. The problem was that sales soared through the roof in the lead up to Christmas, but then plummeted in January and February. This makes sense based on my experience. People go wild for Christmas and then play financial catch-up until April. In order to increase sales in January, toy stores tried two strategies: they lowered prices and they intensified their marketing efforts. However, neither of those tactics worked. Toy stores then tried a third, quite special, strategy.

Every year there are a few toys that become the *big* toys of the season. When I was young it was Scalextric. Other notable Christmas fad toys include Cabbage Patch Doll, Furbie, Tamagotchi, Guitar Hero and Nintendo Wii. Every year, toy stores heavily market these products because they know that in November, when a child sees it on TV, they're likely to ask Mummy and Daddy to buy it for them for Christmas. Many parents make the commitment, *'OK, beautiful child, you will receive said gift from Santa.'* Then, disaster strikes. The store sells out of the fad toy. It's a parent's nightmare. They've made a promise to their child. What do they do? They over-compensate – they buy other expensive toys from the store so that when their child wakes up on Christmas morning they'll not be utterly devastated.

Let's say the parent gets through Christmas relatively unscathed. They feel quite smug watching their child play nicely with the second-choice toys. Then, in January, the whole family are watching TV and guess what they see? Commercials advertising the original fad toy the child was promised, the one that was out of stock shortly before Christmas. The child reminds the parent about their promise. Now the parent is stuck between a rock and a hard place. Either they go to the store and buy the toy (which is a kick in the teeth after already having spent too much money over the Christmas period) or they don't buy the toy for their child (who therefore learns that it's OK to not keep promises and grows up to be a wrong'un). The parent, of course, buys the toy, which means that toy companies maintain sales in January and February (and without dropping prices).

How was this all possible? The toy stores drew upon a principle of influence to help them: commitment. Specifically, we human beings tend to act in a way that's consistent with what we've said in the past. By heavily advertising their fad toy in November, the toy stores created a situation where parents were likely to commit to buying it. Then, the toy stores got sneaky. Despite knowing how many of these toys they'll need in order to satisfy demand (I'd assume they have mathematical geniuses making calculations for them), the toy stores, every year, run out of stock. Do you think that's a coincidence? Of course it isn't. The toy stores were undersupplying over the Christmas period so they could cash in on parental commitment during the slump months of January and February. It's very clever, and I was astounded when I first read about it in Cialdini's book.

Why does it work? It's because people who keep commitments are valued in society, and therefore it has become like a cognitive short cut for how we act in the world. However, often we keep commitments in a somewhat automatic fashion even when it isn't in our best interest to do so. If you go out into the world, you'll see plenty of people exploit this quirk of human behaviour to increase the chances of persuasion.

And now you can use it in university. Let's think about a setting you're likely to encounter, namely, living in close proximity with other people in student digs. If one of those people isn't washing up after themselves, how could you use this principle? Well, make them go on record, *'Olivia, I know you're busy right now, but promise me you'll do the dishes later?'* If Olivia makes the promise then she'll be more likely to do the dishes, and all of a sudden, you'll find yourself in a better (and cleaner) social environment.

Reciprocity – 'But I owed her'

If someone does something for us, we tend to feel obliged to return the favour. On the other hand, if you do something for someone else they'll owe you.

A classic study was conducted on this topic in the 1970s. The researchers asked two participants to rate a piece of art, but one of the participants was a plant (although the visual of a human plant is hilarious, here I mean that s/he was part of the experiment). In one condition, the plant left the experiment and returned with a gift for the participant (a fizzy drink they had bought from a vending machine). In a second condition, the plant returned with nothing for the participant. Later on in the experiment, the plant asked participants from both conditions if they would be willing to buy some raffle tickets. Participants who had earlier received a free fizzy drink from the plant bought twice as many raffle tickets as those who had received nothing. Take-home message: when someone does something for us, we feel obliged to do something for them in return.

You can use this principle in the real world easily enough. If you work in a restaurant be sure to add a mint to the tray when delivering the bill; if you want to get some-one's number in a nightclub be sure to buy them a drink first (provided they don't run away before you can get to them); or if you want your dad to take you out to practise driving be sure to make him a cup of coffee before you ask.

You can use it in university too. Imagine you're doing something that many students dread: groupwork. Imagine that your group was given a task to complete and that you wanted to take control of a certain sub-task. In such situations it can be hard to get what you want, but reciprocity may be able to help. For example, walking into your first group meeting with a bag of doughnuts may do wonders.

You could even use the rule of reciprocity with our friend Olivia, *'I read your assignment Olivia, any chance you can clean the kitchen?'* This example is a good one for illustrating three other things worth knowing about this principle:

1. The person who becomes obliged doesn't have to ask for the favour in the first place. Olivia will still feel like she owes you even if she didn't ask for your help with the assignment.

2. The exchange can be unequal. Olivia's dishes may take significantly longer to do than the amount of time you spend looking at the assignment.

3. The rule can be extended to concession. If you're seen to make a compromise in a negotiation, then the other party will likely make a compromise too. For example, imagine you wanted Olivia to clean the kitchen. Firstly, you ask Olivia to clean the kitchen and the bathroom. After Olivia says *'No'* you then ask her to clean only the kitchen. Olivia is more likely to say *'Yes'* to your second request than if you would have just asked her to clean the kitchen in the first place. Why? Because you made a compromise from your initial position, Olivia will probably

repay that compromise with a compromise of
her own.

Liking – 'But I really liked him'

People we like tend to be able to persuade us, so if you can
make yourself likeable then there's a better chance that
you'll get what you want. But how do we become more
likeable? There are some simple ways:

- By improving how physically attractive we are. As
  horrific as this is, the *halo effect* means that we tend
  to like people who are good-looking or nicely pruned.
  (Note: I laboured over whether I should include this
  point, as I wouldn't want students making drastic
  decisions about their appearance as a result of my
  book. But I included it because what I'm talking about
  here is doing the best with what we've got, which we
  all can do.)
- By being similar to the person we're trying to persuade. Salesmen will often do anything to build
  common ground with their customers.
- By being cooperative. We tend to like people who
  seem to be on our side e.g., *'Let me just argue with
  my boss about this so I can get you the best deal.'*
- By being complimentary (as Cialdini puts it, we're
  phenomenal suckers for flattery).

I find being complimentary the easiest of those techniques

to use in everyday life because it seems to improve the chances of persuasion even when the compliment isn't true. I was on the receiving end of this not too long ago when a charity representative knocked at my door. The conversation went as follows, *'Hi there, my name is Jaime and I'm seeking donations for* [insert charity here].' I replied with the same indifference that most people probably do, *'Uh huh.'* At the time, Jaime's next question seemed like a plausible one to ask, but looking back on the situation I see no reason why he would need this information from me, *'Would you mind me asking how old you are?'* It's difficult to decline a request like this in normal discourse, so I answered, *'I'm thirty-five.'* Jaime quickly jumped in with, *'Wow, you look young for your age.'*

And there it was. Jaime was exploiting one of the easiest ways to influence people. He set up the situation in order to pay me a compliment. Interestingly enough, over the years, numerous friends have commented on how I look much older than I actually am, and yet here was Jaime, on a day when I had a full beard and was wearing my dressing gown after a morning of marking, telling me the opposite. Now you'd think that being a lecturer of psychology, whose job it is to teach about influence, that I'd have spotted the tactic. And I did, sort of. But it made no difference. That's the thing about being complimentary: people appreciate it even if they know the compliment is false. It's almost like a magic trick, and well worth adding to your collection of social skills.

Social proof – 'But that's what everyone else is doing'

In situations where we don't know the correct course of action, we tend to follow the behaviour of other people. There's a brilliant study that illustrates this principle. The researchers asked a plant (ha!) to stand on a pavement in New York and look up at the side of a tall building. They then measured how many passers-by stopped and looked up at the side of the building too. Not many passers-by did. However, in the second condition, five plants were now looking up at the side of the building. Soon twenty to thirty new people had joined the five plants and had absolutely no idea what they were looking at. What does this show? The more people that are doing something, the more likely we are to see that as the right behaviour in a given situation.

Like all the principles I've told you about, following them works a lot (but not all) of the time (this is why they became principles in the first place). In the case of social proof, copying other people in most situations is a functional thing to do. For example, if you see a bunch of people running through the university canteen with a panicked look on their faces, then your best bet is probably to run with them despite the fact that you won't know what you're running from. However, knowing that human beings tend to look to others for information about how to act is like gold to people who want to persuade, because all they have to do is to structure a situation so that the following message reaches the person they're trying to influence: *everyone is doing this.*

You can see this principle in everyday life without looking too hard. For example, bartenders put their own money in a tip jar at the beginning of the night, nightclub owners keep queues outside their nightclub even when there's no one inside, and people often choose who they follow on social media based on how many followers a person has, rather than the quality of their content.

There's even a lovely story about the person who invented the shopping trolley that draws on social proof. Sylvan Goldman invented the trolley for his supermarket in Oklahoma City because he could see shoppers struggling to carry heavy baskets (although the cynic in me assumes Goldman knew that trolleys would enable shoppers to carry more and therefore spend more money). However, when it was first introduced, shoppers avoided taking advantage of this strange-looking contraption because it was unfamiliar. As a result, Goldman paid models to use his shopping trolley, which prompted others to do so as well.

When I was a student, I used to employ social proof to jump-start a night out. I would approach a bunch of friends individually and tell them the names of all the other people going out (I did this without confirming with those other people that they were actually going). I'd then tell them how the nightclub we were planning on going to had a million five-star ratings. That was usually enough to persuade people to get involved.

Expert authority – 'But she told me to do it'

We're more likely to be persuaded to do stuff by people in positions of authority (we tend to listen to doctors, teachers, politicians, etc.). This tactic usually pays off (doctors understand more than we do and so we trust them when they tell us things). However, knowing that we tend to follow the instructions of people who have authority means that if we can create merely the *appearance* of authority, we'll be able to increase the chances of persuasion.

A classic study was conducted on this topic. In one condition, a plant (who was dressed normally) asked a passer-by to give some money to a person struggling to pay for a parking meter. Levels of persuasion in this condition were low. However, in the second condition, persuasion was much higher. How? The plant was now dressed as a policeman. Merely the appearance of authority increased persuasion. (Note: impersonating a police officer is against the law, so best not to try this at home.)

There are ways that you could use this principle in everyday life, but the urban myth that I love goes like this. A man dressed in a uniform and armed with an *Admission* sign worked for years accepting payment from people for parking outside a UK zoo. One day, a zoo customer asked a member of staff, *'Where's that nice man who runs the car park?'* The member of staff replied with, *'What man? Parking is free at the zoo.'* All it took was the appearance of authority.

You could use this principle in university, if you think about it carefully enough. For example, dressing in smart attire will make people listen to you more (including lecturers), and referencing authorities when arguing will help you to win those arguments (e.g., *'I understand your point but Dr Roberta Delve, who's the international expert on baked beans, says otherwise.'*).

Scarcity – 'But they were running out'

When things are becoming unavailable, we tend to want them more. In other words, the value of an item changes depending on its availability rather than its inherent quality. You'll see this tactic used plenty in the selling of products (e.g., *'Only five cars like this one are left in the UK'* or *'Eight people are viewing this coffee machine'*). TV shopping was built on this principle. On the side of the screen there's a counter showing the product becoming less available as people supposedly buy it.

The best story I've heard that taps into the scarcity principle goes like this. Let's imagine that someone wants to buy a washing machine. The customer visits a store and approaches a washing machine in which they're mildly interested. Michelle, the salesperson, then informs the customer that the washing machine ran out of stock a few days ago. The customer seems disappointed at this piece of news – the washing machine has become more attractive since becoming unavailable. Michelle then says, *'You know what, let me just go out to the stock room and check that we don't have one hiding somewhere.'* Michelle goes to the stock room and, in the presence of twenty-five of the *unavailable* washing machines, plays *Candy Crush* for a few minutes. She returns to the customer and says that she has found one last washing machine. At this point, not only is it tricky for the customer to say *'No'*, given that Michelle has spent time trying to help them, but also the customer will feel delighted that the thing they thought unavailable has become available. And all of this happened because of the scarcity principle.

This principle, in my opinion, is most useful in an important domain of your university life: romantic partners. Acting unavailable to potential partners will make you seem more attractive than you actually are – and who wouldn't want that?

Is it wrong to know about (and use) these principles?

And there you have it: the six principles of persuasion. I like to teach my students about them for a few reasons:

1. This is the sort of stuff that students usually got into psychology for in the first place. They watched *The Mentalist* or *White Collar* and thought that they'd like to learn how to do it.

2. The principles can be illustrated with cool research from the early days of psychology. It was a bit like the Wild West back then – you could get away with doing anything.

3. The principles are useful in helping my students function in their wider social world more effectively. In fact, I explicitly encourage my students to use these principles on their lecturers. You may want to consider this also. For example, you could make your lecturer promise to help you with a later task (commitment), you could take a coffee for them to a meeting (reciprocity), or you could tell them how much you love their research (liking). It's easy to fit these principles into your life when you stop to think about them.

'Hang on there, Nic,' I hear you say (therefore upsetting my flow for a second time in this chapter), *'Doesn't all of this amount to manipulation?'* Well, yes, sort of. I prefer to think of it as *outcome engineering* but there's no doubt that people with admirable ethical standards might suggest that teaching methods of influence is questionable. However, I would say a couple of things in response. Firstly, influence is everywhere and if you can't spot it, then you've already lost. Secondly, we don't get to choose scientific principles. They exist whether we like it or not. What we can choose, however, is how to use them. It's a bit like this: a chainsaw can be useful, but in the wrong hands it can be deadly. In other words, people can use these powers for good, or they can use them to be an arsehole. I'd go for the former if you want to be able to sleep at night.

A chainsaw can be useful

To conclude this section on persuasion then, we human beings connect in thousands of interactions throughout our lives. During many of these interactions, all parties, whether they know it or not, are trying to influence each other in various ways. If you know the aforementioned principles then you'll be able to manage social relationships more effectively, which will have a knock-on effect with regard to your psychological wellbeing (provided that you don't use the chainsaw in a way that stops you from sleeping at night).

Gangstas' paradise

Now that we've covered the psychology of influence, we're going to take an interesting turn within the topic of human relationships by talking about a barrier that often stops us from connecting with people. And it all comes down to our views about why human beings become the human beings they become. Yes, you're correct: following the light-hearted and straightforward topic of influence, we're about to get deep.

After I finished my time at the University of Kent, I moved to Northern Cyprus to take a lecturing position. What many of you probably don't know is that Northern Cyprus isn't recognised as a legal country by any other country in the world apart from Turkey (I won't go into the history of how that happened, but it's thought-provoking if you ever get the chance to read about it). When I was there this had many implications, but what matters in this particular story is that it had implications for criminals. Specifically, as other countries didn't recognise Northern Cyprus as a legitimate country, many extradition treaties had been rejected. This meant that if a criminal could make it to the northern part of Cyprus, they were somewhat safe. Although there are lots of stories I could tell you about my time there, the experience that impacted me the most involved my relationship with two of these criminals.

I knew all about the first criminal. Let's call her *Charlotte*. Charlotte was prosecuted in another country for some extremely questionable activities and sentenced to spend a long time in prison. She fled and had been on the run ever since, and the Welshman in me is delighted that my first introduction to Charlotte happened in a bar while I held a cold pint of *Efes*. The second criminal was a dog-walking friend named Adrian, who was a fugitive in Northern Cyprus after having been prosecuted for running a multi-million-dollar criminal enterprise. I remember bumping into Adrian on a dog walk the day after an exposé article came out (prior to this I had no idea of his history). I was pooping myself, but Adrian was cool about it. The conversation went like this:

> *'Shouldn't you be in hiding or something?'* I asked, after having watched my fair share of fugitive movies.
>
> *'Yes, I'm just thinking about where. You know something? I got a twenty-five-year sentence, but I didn't rape anyone or kill anyone. I was*

running a business. When I got caught, I accepted it, as I always knew there would be that risk. I began the sentence and I sat there for ten years and waited. But nothing changed. The rapists and the murderers were completing their sentences early, and I sat still. This is despite the fact that they took every bit of income I'd ever made, tens of millions of dollars. While this was happening, I was missing my kids' lives. So, one day, when I was on a weekend release, I ran. And here is where I ended up. I've brought my kids over and now I get to see them every day.'

My reply was a true reflection of how I felt at the time, and not just made up to make Adrian like me in what was a delicate situation. *'I totally understand. I'd have done the same thing. You only live once and if I had the chance to see my kids grow up and if I had the opportunity to live as a free man, then I would be where you are.'*

Although I don't condone Adrian's criminal actions, I still agree with my reply. If I were in his exact situation, with his exact history, I probably would have made the same decision (remember I said that). Following the breaking of the news story, Adrian was hounded by local police and subsequently went into hiding. While Adrian was in hiding, Charlotte mentioned that she needed help installing a new printer, so I made my way up to her villa. This task took longer than I thought it would, so I was there longer than I should have been.

While I was sat at the computer, six men entered Charlotte's house and held a meeting about five yards from me. Charlotte introduced them to me – I don't remember their names, but afterwards I did assign them old American gangster names like *Frankie Four Fingers*. These men were dodgy, they looked mean and they spoke as I would expect gangster types to speak. Put it this way: they would have fitted into any Guy Ritchie movie with no problem. As they entered, I shook their hands and nodded in as tough a way as I could. I then kept my head down and installed the printer. You know how, when you take a driving test, you have to exaggerate looking in the mirrors? Well, I was exaggerating installing this printer, but as they were so close it was impossible not to hear what they were saying.

They began to talk about Adrian. Apparently, he was moving around Northern Cyprus trying to evade the police. However, he could only keep it up for so long before they would find him. Therefore, the gangsters had to figure out a way to help Adrian escape the country. After much deliberation, they decided that they could get him off the island by plane. Don't ask me how they planned to do this – I saw all sorts of logistical problems with the idea, but who was I to advise these gangster folk on their criminal activities? The problem they had, however, as criminals on the run themselves, was that they didn't own credit cards so couldn't make online transactions.

I could have interjected and provided them with my credit card to solve their problem. But I didn't. After several months of knowing Charlotte, I'd seen that the life of a criminal wasn't for me. However, while basking in the relief of knowing that my future didn't involve dangerous and risky illegal activity, I heard the following words come from the circle of gangsters, *'Does Nic have a credit card?'* Fear descended on me. It would be difficult to say *'No'* – but on the other hand, imagine trying to explain this to Amy. She would kill me if she knew I was buying flights for fugitives. All six of them walked over to me, *'Nic, we have a slight problem. None of us has a credit card, but we need one to buy a flight. Any chance you could lend us your credit card?'* Time sort of stood still. I didn't move. I could hear my cousin's voice in my head from a conversation we'd had only a couple of weeks prior, *'Nic, hanging out with criminals will, somewhere down the line, invariably lead to you being complicit or involved in criminal behaviour.'* Harrison was about to be proved right. And then it happened. At that moment, a moment that was potentially life changing, a female voice interrupted before I could say anything, *'Nic isn't getting involved in this.'*

Light can come from unexpected places

Charlotte saved me. Charlotte, a fugitive on the run for some seriously questionable activities. I left the villa feeling relieved, but more importantly, I almost immediately appreciated the fact that I'd just been taught a couple of big lessons about human beings.

Lesson number 1   What often gets in the way of our ability to connect with others is that we effortlessly hold negative attitudes and judgements. That is, we have a tendency to distrust some others on the basis that they might pose a threat to us and simultaneously we tend to trust our own predictions for how those others will behave. We then tend to act accordingly, by staying away from them, and warning everyone else that we know to do the same. Making character judgements in this way is a functional thing to do because it protects us, and those around us, from other people. The problem is that being like this also distances us from other people. It stops us from really *seeing* them.

It certainly made me wary of getting too close to Charlotte. My mind had made judgements about her and subsequent predictions for her behaviour that were worrying. Why? Because on paper, and according to rumour, Charlotte was a bad egg. But then, shockingly, in the moment where it mattered the most, all of my preconceptions were proved wrong. Charlotte showed more courage, honour and care than the majority of people I'd met in my life. Light, in this situation, emerged from what seemed like an unlikely place, and if it can emerge from Charlotte, who was so easy to judge, then it can emerge from anyone.

From this experience, I learned that giving too much weight to my judgements is a waste of time because not only can they be inaccurate or incomplete, but they can also stop me from connecting with people. Consequently, I've been on high alert to any judgemental or negative attitudes I might hold about other people ever since my time with Charlotte, and instead I try to give everyone the benefit of the doubt.

I tell you what: when you live in a world where you look for the light in people, it's a much nicer place to live (even if you get stung sometimes). Indeed, research confirms these ideas. Although judging other people is unavoidable, those people who are aware of their judgements, and hold them lightly, will have better mental health. So, when you next find yourself in the presence of a classmate, housemate or workmate who rubs you up the wrong way, see if you can hold your judgement about their character lightly until you gather more information.

Lesson number 2   There's something else going on here that's crucial to explain because it powers my *don't judge others* rule. Charlotte taught me that people are a product of their experiences. She led the life she did because of the experiences that she had been exposed to. If you or I were exposed to those exact same experiences, then we would have been in a similar place to her. We would be her. Therefore, who are we to judge other people when we haven't walked even one day in their shoes?

As you read those words, they'll make sense to you intellectually, but you may not, right now, understand how profound the implications are of taking this position. If you see every person you meet as a product of their learning

Look for the light in people

experiences, then judgemental attitudes will struggle to have power over you. Why? Because judgemental attitudes are often bolted together by the assumption that there's something inherently wrong with people based on fixed characteristics that are independent of their history. That's a big sentence, but it's an important one. The opposite perspective is that if a person is *bad* then, in some respects, they have little choice in that because their learning history led them there.

Taking this position is really useful when it comes to connecting with people. It means that the actions of all human beings become more understandable because they're linked to histories that any of us could have had. This is why I asked you to remember my response to Adrian. Adrian is another easy character to judge, but by taking the position that people are a product of their experiences, I was able to hold my judgement lightly, and instead just genuinely listen. If you can manage this, to listen with an open mind rather than hold on too tightly to your judgements, then what's left? Understanding, empathy, compassion, love and other such qualities that are only going to help you to connect with people in this world.

Digging into this more

These ideas can be extended in many ways, the most important of which concerns group level processes that blight the human race (prejudice, stereotype, stigma and discrimination). Judgemental and negative attitudes attached to entire groups of people (based on race, sexuality, class or gender, for example) don't make any sense given that the people within those groups may have had totally different life experiences that led them to be who they are.

To say this another way, I know people who have done good things and people who have done bad things, and I'm inclined to think that the good and bad behaviours of those people are a result of their individual histories, rather than their membership of a particular group. From this position, prejudice can't survive. People are the way they are because of where they have been, irrespective of any characteristics they have that might make them targets for abuse.

You can also extend these ideas to the stigma that can come with mental health problems. Have you ever thought about the difference between someone with bad mental health versus someone with good mental health? The go-to answer is biology. But as I mentioned in Chapter 1, there are no reliable biological differences between those two groups of people (and don't tell me you think it's anything to do with serotonin because that's a myth I don't have time to tell you about right now, but look up Robert Whitaker's work if you're interested). And then we come across research showing that poorer people have significantly worse mental health than wealthier people. And it blows our mind because we immediately see that context led the person in question to have the mental health problem (life is significantly tougher psychologically when you don't have money to feed your family).

Back to stigma: should we stigmatise someone for having a mental health problem when what caused it in the first place was being exposed to various (often random) life events that we may not have lived ourselves? Of course not – and when we manage to see people in this way then compassion and empathy and understanding and human connection all become easier. Not only that, but if past context led a person to be the way they are then the present context can help to shape them for the better in the future. So, this is a message of hope. No one is beyond help because if contexts caused the problem in the first place then contexts can always change.

Imagine that you're with me up to this point (any human behaviour is understandable because it emerged out of learning experiences) – now your propensity for connecting with people, all people, has grown exponentially. As an example, at university you'll often see friction between people of different socio-economic classes. We notice someone with a particular accent, we see what they wear, we hear their views and our minds automatically jump into judgement mode. However, if we can see such people as the product of their history then we can, at least, understand them a little more, and perhaps this understanding will give us the space to *see* them as fellow human beings.

The take-home

In this chapter, I couldn't give you a straightforward *connect with people* rule, because a rule like that makes it seem too simple, when the reality is that we operate in a complex social world. Instead, I covered two topics with you. The first was a fun look at some practical tools of influence, which may come in handy when managing wider social relationships.

However, the second topic was much more important. I gave you a rationale as to why you should allow yourself to connect with anyone that you choose. All human beings, whatever their behaviour, are products of their historical (personal and genetic) and current context, and hence all judgemental and negative attitudes can be held lightly because of the realisation that the only difference between you and a criminal is that you've been lucky enough to have the experiences you've had.

It really is a wonderful position to take (and it is a *position* chosen for pragmatic purposes, rather than a truth that can be proved) because it will bring you a lovely sense of humility. You'll appreciate, no matter what you do, that there's nothing inherently special about you – you were just blessed, or not blessed, as you grew up. This sense of humility will draw people towards you such that you may even become a beacon of light for those who are downtrodden. Therefore, take the opportunity to connect with human beings. Be aware that you haven't seen life through their eyes, and that although you might not understand other people's choices, you do understand that their history led them to where they are. Hear their stories. Actively listen. From this place, you'll be able to appreciate diversity and the positive role it can play in shaping you. You'll be able to promote equality. You'll be able to see light in all people and you'll be able to help them see it in themselves too.

Chapter 4 Tasks

Task 1 – Practising persuasion

I want you to think about the context that ties together all the people reading this book. At university, how can the principles of influence help you? Pull up that notes page on your smartphone and write down four concrete things you can do to bring these things to life. I'll give you some examples:

1. *I could give a lecturer a compliment at the end of a session. This would make me memorable and likeable, and therefore increase the chances that the lecturer will help me in the future.*

2. *I could ask someone to 'watch my stuff' when I'm settled in the library but need the toilet. Asking someone to make this commitment means that they will, in all likelihood, follow through with it.*

3. *I could ask a load of people to 'like' a product that I'm selling on Facebook. By doing this, the potential consumer will see that lots of other people like my product and therefore will be more likely to buy it.*

4. *I could give a housemate a bar of chocolate before asking for a lift to the supermarket.*

*Obviously, I'll try not to make what I'm
doing too obvious.*

Task 2 – Looking for light

Unfortunately, a ten-times criminal is likely to
become an eleven-times criminal. These patterns
of behaviour, which are learned over time, are
significant and they rightly inform us to be careful
with people in our social environment. To be clear
about this, although people are built from their
histories and therefore deserve our understanding,
they can still hurt us in the present moment. Indeed,
judgements evolved to keep us safe. The issue is over-
generalisation, whereby our judgement of a person
blocks us from seeing anything else about them.

I'd like you to use this opportunity to find light
in the people around you, and you can do this by
asking the right questions. Over the next week, and
with people that you may have judged negatively in
the past, find a way to work some of the questions
below into the conversation. Leave your thoughts
about completing this exercise on your notes page. In
particular, I want you to record whether you learned
anything surprising about the people you spoke to.
(Note: you may also want to put these questions
to people you know pretty well, as it will bring you
closer to them.)

▲ *Where did you grow up? What was that like?*

▲ *What were your parents like?*

▲ *Who was your best friend? What were they like? Do you still see them?*

▲ *What are your best and worst memories of being a teenager?*

▲ *Do you miss home now you're at university?*

▲ *Who do you miss the most and why?*

▲ *What do you want to do after university?*

▲ *Do you have any big dreams?*

▲ *If you could achieve anything, what would it be?*

▲ *What would you do if you were rich?*

▲ *Who has taught you the most in life, and what did they teach you?*

▲ *What makes a person strong?*

▲ *When did you feel the worst you have felt?*

▲ *When was the last time you cried?*

▲ *What do you hope people will remember about you once you're dead and gone?*

Chapter 5

Give to Others

The helper's high

There are plenty of ways to give to other people, but in my opinion they fall into two main categories: our time and our money. Many people give away their time or their money with the aim of changing the life, even in a small way, of the person they're giving it to. However, research shows that the person who does the giving also gains a significant amount, in terms of their psychological and physical health.

Let's start with giving our time. People who volunteer, people who help out with community activities, and even people who commit to one act of kindness per week for six weeks show improved psychological wellbeing (in terms of happiness, life satisfaction, self-esteem, etc.). One study showed that people actually have higher levels of happiness and satisfaction after engaging in philanthropic activities, relative to engaging in activities that they find to be fun. Moreover, giving our time to people in the form of social support is associated with increases in wellbeing and oxytocin, and decreases in depression, blood pressure, cortisol and mortality rates (one study, as unlikely as it sounds, showed that offering social support to others had a life-lengthening effect on people with AIDS).

In addition to time, we can also give away our money. Research shows that financial generosity leads to better emotional wellbeing (this goes for rich people and for poor people), and that across cultures, human beings are happier when they spend their money on other people relative to spending money on themselves. Giving to charity also positively impacts psychological wellbeing, even when (1) the gifter doesn't know who's receiving their donation and (2) the gifter knows that nobody else will find out about the fact that they've made a donation. The simple act of giving matters that much.

The advice thus far is straightforward. If you want to improve your own wellbeing then find a way to build giving behaviour, in the form of time or money, into your life on a continuing basis. However, for the most part in this chapter I want to discuss a different and less straightforward form of giving, which builds on Chapter 4's focus on human relationships. What I'm talking about is how, in life, there'll be some people who we *give ourselves* to, or *give our love* to. Although this action is a fundamental part of being a human being, many people run away from it, in various ways, because of the hurt that it can bring.

Dressing up with old men

Let me tell you something not many people know about me. I used to be a freemason. No, that doesn't mean that I did naughty things with animals or that I ruled the world. Despite enjoying the odd moment of feeding the mystery that surrounds it, the truth is that freemasonry is a lot less exciting than people think. After entering the society via a friend or family member (for me, it was my grandad), a prospective freemason might expect secrets and influence, but what they quickly find out is that freemasonry mostly involves charity and learning. Like I said, it's not that exciting.

Consequently, when freemasons realise that they're not being offered better jobs or getting ahead, many ask themselves this question, *'Why do I persist with this peculiar commitment?'* For me the answer was simple: it gave me the opportunity to connect with people from the older generation. It allowed me to bask in the wisdom of sixty-to-ninety-year-old men (yes, I was the youngest, and the most physically stable, by quite some distance), and I think I'll forever appreciate the fact that I had that opportunity. However, the problem with a lodge full of older men is that death is a piece of the furniture. For example, in my six-month stint in freemasonry, three friends passed away. At their funerals I was upset, but not uncontrollably so. I guess this was because although these men were my friends, I wasn't close enough to them for their deaths to impact my life in any major way.

However, there were people at those funerals for whom this was not the case. At their funerals, and at every funeral

I've been to, marital partners, brothers, sisters, children, grandchildren, cousins and life-long friends appear heart-broken. Although sometimes people dress up funerals as a celebration, the sense of loss and hurt is consistently the major thing that I see.

I guess this all sounds like doom and gloom, but the remarkable and beautiful thing about funerals is that *hurt* isn't the only feeling on show, because it's tightly tied to another crucial emotion for human beings. *Love* is also there, hiding beneath the surface. I like to think of the relationship between the two as being like this. Imagine that we each have a coin. On one side of the coin it says *Love*. This side represents the way in which we give ourselves to other people in the service of loving connection. On the other side of the coin, however, there's *Hurt*. By allowing ourselves to love, we leave ourselves vulnerable. Put simply, people are hurting at funerals because they gave their love to someone who's now lost to them.

The unfortunate thing about this situation is the inevitability of hurt once we give away our love. What do I mean by this? There are three angles worth discussing:

1. The people we love, in this tricky world, will trip up and hurt themselves, and when we see this happen, we'll feel their hurt too. When you give your love to someone, you inhabit a life where the experiences of that person are intimately tied to your own well-being. If something happens to them then something happens to you.

2. Sometimes the people that we give our love to can no longer be close to us (they leave our lives out of choice or by necessity). When this happens, we're likely to feel pretty rubbish about it.

3. Hurt will always have the ace in the hole. Even if the people we love live in a way that's close to us, and live lives devoid of tragedy (which is very unlikely), then we still won't be free from hurt because one day we'll see them die (provided that we don't die first).

So what this basically means is that, provided we give away our love, every day we live we move one day closer to tragedy. The bottom line is that hurt and love go together – they're two sides of the same coin.

Love and hurt are two sides of the same coin

All we need is love

Wow! I'm not doing much better at being positive here, but I reckon I can turn things around.

Giving someone your love is a wonderful thing. For example, if you asked me to describe my major reason for being alive, my answer would be something to do with the people I give my love to, and I'm sure that you would say the same. We really would not live our lives to the full if we didn't give ourselves to other people in this way. However, we can't do this without acknowledging that arguably the most positive aspect of human life also brings us ultimate vulnerability. We can't both give ourselves to someone else and expect not to be hurt if they experience distress, or if we lose them. We can't have one side of our love/hurt coin without having the other.

In some sense, I think we all know this. And yet, once someone we love hurts us in some form, we start to question whether it's worth loving people at all. For example, if you fall in love with someone and they dump you, you may start to regret falling in love in the first place. If your best friend moves to another country, the hurt may provoke you to be more careful about making friends in the future. And if someone you love dies, the thought may cross your mind that it would have been better never to have met that person, than to experience the unbearable hurt of losing them forever.

Once we've been hurt like this our mind will start devising a strategy to protect us from the pain that other people can bring to our lives. And it will come up with a solution. We just avoid love. We throw away the coin. We step away from loving connection but, more importantly, we protect ourselves from painful feelings. Many of us take or have taken this approach. We don't love because we're scared of being hurt. And in doing this we make a huge mistake. Therefore, the question arises, if giving our love to other people is important, how can we go about doing this while managing the inevitable hurt that comes with it? For me, there's only one answer: *acceptance*.

Let's talk about acceptance

Pursuing a full, rich and meaningful life while accepting the pain and struggles that come with it would seem like a fair deal. But whereas most of us are fine about the first half of that trade-off we're generally less keen about the second half. That makes sense, as no one wants to experience hurt. Yet here's the truth – if we're going to live a fulfilling life, then we can't avoid difficult feelings. If we want the ups, then we have to be prepared for the downs. We can't have one without the other. This is easy to say and understand, but living it is hard.

If you want ups, be prepared for downs

A metaphor that I like to use to illustrate acceptance is called *The Unwelcome Guest*. It goes something like this.

Meet Duncan. He wants to have a party with his friends and enjoy himself. He also wants all his guests to have a good time, and finds himself feeling anxious about this. His heart starts to race and his mind wonders, *'Will people come?'*, *'Are people enjoying themselves?'* and *'Do people think I'm boring, would they rather be talking with someone else?'*

Just when the party is in full flow, an unwelcome guest, Freddy, shows up. Duncan doesn't really like Freddy and doesn't want him to be there. And since his arrival, Duncan has felt Freddy's been ruining the party. Duncan asks him to leave but he won't go away, so instead Duncan ushers Freddy into a back room and guards the door in an effort to keep him away from the other guests. Only now Duncan is missing out on the party too. He longs to re-join it but knows that Freddy will follow him and that's the last thing he wants to happen.

The metaphor is that Freddy, the unwelcome guest, is like Duncan's feeling of anxiety. Duncan tries to get rid of or control this feeling but, like Freddy, it just won't leave. Of course, all the time and effort he puts into trying not to feel anxious means he's less engaged with the party and what's going on around him. What can Duncan do? Well, one option is to welcome Freddy into the party. Duncan will still feel annoyed but at least he can be with his friends rather than wasting his time trying to keep Freddy out.

This is what acceptance means. Rather than trying to get rid of unwanted feelings, acceptance involves inviting them in, and making a space for them in our lives.

A miracle cure

When people learn that acceptance is a useful tool for responding to difficult feelings, they sometimes start to throw it around like it's an easy answer to the world's problems. In some ways, I guess that's what bugs me about acceptance – it can be misleading. It can be sold as a valiant superhero, equipped to take away human suffering in one swift blow. Yet when acceptance is thought of in this quick-psychological-fix sort of way, it's more like one of those salesmen from black-and-white cowboy movies who drive from town to town selling miracle cures. Acceptance can deceive people into thinking that it's a miracle cure for difficult feelings. But it isn't.

If you ever hear someone paint acceptance as an easy thing to achieve, by saying something like, *'Just accept the anxiety'*, then do watch the face of the person they're talking to. Usually, it will contort in such a way as if to say, *'What does that even mean?'* It's a good question. What do we really mean by this term? Are we talking about conjuring up a mysterious feeling of acceptance at a moment's notice? Our inner worlds just aren't that simple. I wish it were possible to flick a switch and feel accepting but, much like the feeling of happiness, or any feeling at all really, it's pretty difficult to control.

You might by now be thinking that I'm not a fan of acceptance, but that couldn't be further from the truth. You'd be correct in thinking that I'm not a fan of acceptance in the everyday quick-psychological-fix notion of the word. However, I am most certainly a fan of the way acceptance is meant in the professional waters that I swim in. Let me describe what acceptance refers to in that world.

Introducing willingness

The first thing you need to know about *acceptance* is that most of the psychologists I know never use that word, preferring to use *willingness*. The reason for this is because acceptance sometimes smells of toleration; we'll tolerate the bad feeling until something better comes along. Willingness isn't toleration – it's the active choice to contact something difficult in the service of what's important to us. Think about it: if we head into willingness in order to make a difficult feeling go away then we are, by definition, unwilling. True willingness doesn't mean accepting our feelings on the condition that they'll cease to exist. It means accepting our feelings. Period. It means actively choosing to feel horrible feelings, it means carrying them with us, and taking ownership of them, because doing so will help us to lead a fuller and richer life.

The second, and arguably most important, thing that you need to know about acceptance is that it's not a feeling. Just get your head around that. Feelings are so whimsical. They come and they go like the clouds and they're difficult to control. When we say the words, *'Just accept the anxiety'* the underlying implication is that it's possible to manufacture a feeling of acceptance. There's no doubt that, at times, we do experience the feeling of acceptance, but it's really hard to create on the spot. However, you don't have to *feel* willing in order to *act* willingly. When we talk about willingness, we're talking about acting in a willing way when it would be easier not to. We're talking about becoming friendly with discomfort. For example, if we're craving chocolate while on a diet, then willingness is the action of sitting in a chair, acknowledging the uncomfortable feeling and not moving towards the cupboard. If we're feeling down and lying in bed, then willingness is choosing to get up and go to the shops while feeling rubbish inside.

Are you open to trying this sort of strategy in your own life? If so, you're probably wondering how you might be able to practise it. In my opinion, willingness is easy to practise; all we have to do is to get into a situation that brings us discomfort, choose to have that discomfort, and do what we had planned to do anyway. However, you may be sat down, somewhere in this big world, with a different opinion, *'I still don't see how I can practise willingness. How on Earth do I get myself into a situation that brings me discomfort in my everyday life?'*

My counter argument to that sentiment would look something like this. You probably find yourself in situations that bring you discomfort on most days without having to try too hard; you just don't realise it because avoidance is so embedded into how you operate in the world. What this means is that you'll actually have plenty of opportunities to practise embracing discomfort, if only you open your eyes to it. Just take the chapters we've covered so far as an example of the ubiquity (great word there) of discomfort:

- *Exercise* If you're running a 5k then you're going to reach a time in that run when you experience psychological (and physical) pain. Can you have those feelings and keep running?
- *Challenge yourself* When you fail at a challenge, you're going to feel down on yourself, you may feel stupid and a bit worthless. Can you have those feelings and still take on the next challenge?
- *Connect with people (part 1)* Just before you try a persuasion tactic on someone, you may feel nervous and anxious. Can you have those feelings and continue as planned?
- *Connect with people (part 2)* Sometimes getting to know someone will not go well, and this may make you feel awkward and incapable. Can you have those feelings and try again in the future?

We spend so much time running away from difficult feelings that often we avoid doing things that are important to our wellbeing. Willingness encourages people to contact discomfort in the service of pursuing what's important. If we can do this then our options open right out. If we act to avoid discomforting feelings, think of all the ways in which we limit our life. When we make discomfort our friend, we're able to do so much more, and doing more will result in a richer and more meaningful existence.

In order to get your feet moving with this skill, I'd like you to consider doing some practice right now (notes page, smartphone). I do an exercise with my students where I ask them to stare into each other's eyes for a few minutes, without speaking and without breaking eye contact. This exercise really makes people squirm (which I love to see). See if you can find someone to do this with. When you initially make eye contact, notice the discomfort that you feel, choose and own that discomfort, and maintain eye contact with the person regardless. If you manage to do this then you'll see that it's possible to act willingly even when you feel totally unwilling. And once you know this, you'll be able to practise this skill in various aspects of your life.

Don't throw feedback in the bin

Willingness can come in handy in many situations at university, but I want to mention one area where it may be particularly useful for you. What many students don't fully appreciate is that if they don't develop good academic skills during their degree then they can't get a decent grade. In the social sciences the most important academic skill they'll need to develop is writing. I tell this to my students on day one; I tell them that their degree is as much a writing degree as it is a psychology degree. However, on day one of a degree most students aren't good enough at writing (with respect to the standard expected at university), and so my job is to shape their skills over time. And how do I do that? I give feedback.

Ooooch! Just the word *feedback* is enough to send shivers down the spine of any student. Why? Because feedback can feel cruel. Being told how to do something better implies that what we were doing before wasn't good enough. However, at the same time as causing discomfort, being receptive to feedback is also the only way to improve at basically everything we ever do.

This continues throughout our lives and is ever-present in mine. For example, if a number of students say in their course evaluations that I don't do enough to explain the concepts I teach about, then I know that I have to work on how I explain things (most probably by using more examples). Or if, when I'm writing a research article, a senior collaborator tells me that I use too many colons, then I know to look out for colons in my writing (that exact scenario happened with this book). When we're given feedback by anyone who we trust has the skill to be able to give us good feedback, then it's important to take it on board, even when it hurts. Don't get me wrong – you're allowed to disagree with the feedback, but you must at least consider it first.

I wish I'd known this when I was your age. But I didn't. Whenever I received feedback for an assignment, the first thing I did was to look at the mark. If the mark was low, then I'd rip up the feedback and put it in the bin. What an ignoramus I was (another great word for you there), but I can understand my behaviour now I know what I know. The feedback I received essentially told me that I wasn't good enough (and *how* I wasn't good enough) and therefore brought a shedload of discomfort I didn't want to have. My response to this was to throw away the feedback. This limited my exposure to the discomfort (yay!), but in doing so I also threw away any chance I had at improving (boo!).

During the first two years of my degree I did this sort of thing a lot and, shockingly enough, my marks didn't change. Willingness to experience discomfort would have allowed me to embrace feedback and therefore given me a better chance at developing my skills.

Heck, while we're talking about how being willing can help us to respond better to feedback, I should mention that being willing can also help us to complete assignments in the first place.

What am I talking about here? Well, the process of putting together an assignment can be excruciating. The most common feelings are boredom, confusion, pressure, unintelligence and unworthiness. In fact, the one feeling that I hear of most with regard to completing assignments (with which I fully empathise, based on my experience) is tricky to sum up in one word. It's what I call a *I can't be fucked* feeling. However, if we're unwilling to experience a feeling of apathy such as this then we'll be more likely to take less care with our assignment, and just try to get through it as quickly as we can. If I'm ever unwilling to embrace that *I can't be fucked* feeling, then the resulting work is never something to be proud of.

I'd like to promise you that this all changes as you get

older, but I'm still living it at thirty-five years old, and the best example I can give again concerns this book. Very often as I open my laptop to type words into this document I have the same difficult feelings that I had when completing assignments at university. When those feelings come along, if I'm unwilling to have them, then I'll stop writing and check Twitter instead. If I do this, then in the short term I'll feel great because I avoided the difficult feelings. But if I do this sort of thing too much over time I'll feel awful because I won't be moving towards something that's important to me. I'll wilt away like a flower without water (I hope you appreciate my poetic language there).

As evidenced by the fact that you're reading this book, once you have willingness to experience difficult feelings you get to continue with tasks that are important but not enjoyable, knowing all too well that discomfort is a natural part of the journey. In some ways, willingness to experience difficult feelings and continue while holding them is the very definition of resilience. And being resilient is not only a significant predictor of success but also a great attribute to have in these uncertain days.

Back to love

So now you can see that willingness is a skill that we can use in many different areas of life, and with lots of different types of feelings. However, it's an absolutely crucial skill when it comes to loving relationships. If we're not willing to experience the hurt and vulnerability that can come with giving away our love, then we can't fully give it away in the first place or continue to do so once we're in relationships with people.

But how do we practise willingness in this context? The ideal scenario is that the skill of willingness we develop in our everyday lives will hold steady when it comes to the hurt that other people can bring. I say this because practising willingness in the context of loving relationships is trickier than practising willingness generally. We sort of have to wait until hurt happens and then watch our reaction to see if we start shutting down. For example, if we see someone we love in pain, do we continue to sit by their side as they lie in a hospital bed? Or do we avoid the hospital because of the hurt it brings? And if someone we love leaves or dies, do we continue to give our love to other people knowing that they too will hurt us? Or do we decide that a life on our own will be easier?

Despite it being difficult to practise willingness to experience the discomfort that other people can bring to us, that doesn't mean that we can't imagine how willingness might be a handy skill to have in this domain. With this in mind, let's talk about a pretty exciting thing that can happen during your university adventure: romantic relationships.

Relationship advice

There are two elements to this topic that are worthy of exploration – finding someone and keeping someone.

Without being willing to experience discomfort, we don't get to find someone in the first place. The very nature of *pulling* involves stepping outside of our comfort zone. It involves a fast-beating heart, sweaty palms and a physical shaking of the body. It involves feelings of worry, anxiety and the fear of rejection. If we're unwilling to have those physical sensations and uncomfortable feelings, then we're not even on the start line when the race begins.

As an added bit of advice, if you do see someone you like and plan to approach them, be sure to have a sensible way to break the ice. One of the first times I saw a girl I liked, I thought it would be a good idea to grab her attention by kicking a football close to where she was (to avoid the discomfort of just speaking to her). Unfortunately, this was before I became a good footballer. The ball hit her square in the chest. After the crying stopped, we didn't end up speaking. And I never saw her again.

Anyhow, I digress. Now imagine that you do manage to embrace those feelings and that you ask someone out on a date. And imagine they say *'No'*. How are you then going to feel? Hurt and embarrassed most probably. If you're not willing to have those feelings, then next time there's an opportunity to ask someone out on a date, you won't do it. You'll avoid trying to find someone to give your love to because you'll be unwilling to experience more hurt and embarrassment.

Let's imagine a better outcome to that situation. You ask someone out on a date, and they say *'Yes'*. Happy days! However, now you're in the early stages of a romantic relationship with someone, and you need to try to keep them. The trouble, especially early on, is that the fear of being hurt may drive you to do some silly things. You may be overly suspicious of your partner's behaviour (perhaps you'll start checking their phone) and you may smother them with your attention (making it hard for them to breathe). If you're unwilling to experience the feeling of vulnerability that comes with the possibility of being hurt, then it's more likely that you'll do things that make your relationship suffer, even if that's the last thing you want.

Finally, imagine that you've got through the early high-octane stages of a relationship (you'll know when you've reached this place as the excitement and sex will have slowed down). The next thing you have to do is be willing to accept that your long-term wellbeing is tied to the existence of your relationship. You now have a best friend who's integral to your life. You have to accept the vulnerability that comes with truly letting someone into your inner world, and you have to accept the fact that one day, if you lose them, it's going to hurt like hell. If you're not accepting of those things, then you'll run for the hills when the possibility of long-term commitment comes along.

My 'hurt/love' coin

There are plenty of other relationships where willingness is also important. Let me tell you the major way this has played out for me, by talking about parenthood.

If I were my dad, I'd have given up a long time ago. As a

young man he badly injured his knee playing football, which left him with chronic knee and back pain. Don't let those words just pass over you. My dad has spent most of his days in physical pain, which is enough to fill anyone's bucket. Despite this, he has been the most loving and supportive parent. The sort of parent who played chess and Scrabble with me after a hard day's work. The sort of parent who took me to various hobbies as I grew up. The sort of parent who just listened when I needed someone to listen. The sort of parent who cries with pride and love when he sees me. In short, my dad is my blueprint for how to be a father. However, he's also a bit wrecked, psychologically speaking.

When I was ten years old, my dad was accused of committing a serious crime. It's hard for me to write those words in such a public place because of the cascade of events that followed. Unfortunately, some local media outlets found out about the accusations, which meant that my dad's face was all over the news. My brother and I were quite protected from it. We had experiences around the time (kids saying nasty things) that didn't make sense until a lot later in our lives. Following a few weeks of media frenzy, the Crown Prosecution Service didn't take the case forward due to a lack of evidence and inconsistencies in the accusers' accounts. Nevertheless, twenty-five years ago worker's rights were not protected like they are today. My dad lost his job and was somewhat tarnished as an employment prospect.

He then showed strength that I don't think I would have. He accepted any work at all in order to pay the bills (his major job was as a window cleaner for which he earned a pittance). Despite having worked hard to become qualified for a job that paid good money, my dad had to swallow his pride for the sake of the mortgage. But it wasn't pride, I believe, that caused his psychological troubles, and it breaks my heart to say this. What I think caused my dad's suffering following these events was that in his future he saw nice houses for his family, nice cars for his family, nice holidays for his family and early retirement for his family. In his eyes, the future of the people he cared for the most had been unfairly ripped from him.

Thoughts like that are hard to deal with. Thoughts that you're responsible for your family and you're letting them down, that you wasted years qualifying for a job you can no longer do, that the fulfilment you experienced through your job was something you wouldn't have again, that the people responsible for the decision are flourishing, that everyone in the city would always have doubts about your innocence, and that those people may also harm your children with their words.

What did he do in order to live with these attacks from his own mind? He drank. And it worked to some degree (by drinking he was able to numb the pain). However, in solving the first problem he created a second, much bigger problem. He was no longer as attentive a husband, he had a shorter fuse with his children, he became more socially isolated and he developed alcohol-related health issues. Now this chain of events, at this point in this book, will make total sense to you. Firstly, what's the major thing that can cause people to experience psychological troubles? Difficult life experiences. Therefore, was my dad justified in his suffering? Yes, he was. Secondly, how do people generally deal with psychological troubles? Avoidance. Therefore, was the way that my dad developed a reliance on alcohol abnormal? No, it wasn't.

The problem, however, is that I didn't know about these things when I was growing up. All I saw was a person who I loved in psychological pain. And, in the typical love/hurt coin kind of way, loving someone who was in pain brought me pain. And I really didn't like this pain. So, much to my shame, I threw away the coin. I became distant from my dad (often in the form of anger) because I couldn't stand seeing him in pain. I couldn't *give myself* to him any longer. The cost of that decision, for a while, was that although I protected myself from a certain sort of hurt, I lost loving connection with someone who was very important to me.

Time went on and I became a dad myself, and this love/ hurt coin thing began to play out again. I love my son more than I thought it was possible to love. I love my son so much that the thought of him in pain brings me a pain that I don't know how to handle. But, with my own dad in mind, where does this road lead? Will I one day distance myself from my son in order to protect myself from hurt? Will I play down his worries and anxieties so that I'm not exposed to them myself? Will I make things as easy as possible on him, as he grows up, so that I don't have to see him experience hardship? Would doing any of those things help him or nourish our relationship?

Where willingness leads

Developing my willingness skills has meant that I've been able to reconnect with my dad. For example, upon seeing my dad in pain, it's typical for me to feel terrible. If I'm willing to have that feeling without needing to be rid of it, then I can get on with being supportive. Put more simply, the thought, *'I could spend some time with Dad, but I can't because it would make me feel sad'* has become *'I'm going to spend some time with Dad, even though it may make me feel sad.'* The development of these skills has also allowed me to give myself fully to the most important person in my life, my son. I now understand that my worry is an indicator of my love, and that it's possible to carry this discomfort in my pocket while being 100 per cent there for him. I understand that toning down my love in order to tone down the potential for hurt would likely mean a relationship with less meaning and depth, which is not something that I want.

My guess would be that the story of parenthood I've just told you will strike a chord. Why? For three reasons:

1. Being away from your parents (at university or on some other adventure) is hard. The separation may leave you with feelings of homesickness and may impact your ability to make sense of the world. I hope you'll now see that such feelings occur only because you love these people, and therefore you have every right to miss them. I hope you'll also see, however, that it's possible to hold such feelings while you still chase your dreams.

2. If I love my son with such vigour, then it's likely that your parents love you to a similar degree, and they're probably shitting themselves right now with you being away (or about to go away). With this in mind, feel free to tell them how much you love them. I can promise you that they'll appreciate it.

3. The stories illustrate, in the rawest way, how I live by the principles I'm teaching you about. I'm not some guru bestowing knowledge to you from on high. I'm down in the dirt with you trying to figure it out, and willingness is a skill that I've found to be really helpful.

The take-home

Giving to other people is an important wellbeing behaviour. By giving away our money and our time, we tend to feel better about ourselves. Although this chapter touches on that aspect of giving, the focus quickly moves onto the idea of giving ourselves to others. In life, we all meet some special people to whom we might give our unconditional love. These people will be our parents, grandparents, brothers and sisters, children, friends and romantic partners. This is a beautiful thing, and according to research evidence, such loving connection with the most important people in our lives will bring ultimate fulfilment. However, it can also make us feel vulnerable (if we give someone our heart, then they can break it), which can sometimes stop us from fully giving ourselves to others.

What's the way forward with this? Acceptance.
Acceptance (or willingness) involves taking action, while
bringing difficult feelings with us. As counterintuitive as it
may seem, it can help us to open up to vulnerability, doubt,
pain and a whole host of other unwanted feelings, therefore
allowing us to build meaningful relationships. In this way,
acceptance provides a great tool in managing the hurt that
can happen when we give someone our love. If I were to
break this down into a soundbite of wisdom, I'd say this:
giving your love to others in life is key to healthy psychological functioning, and the key to truly giving away your
love is willingness.

When you're willing, you give yourself to others knowing
that when hurt comes along, you can have it and continue
loving. Willingness allows you to choose hurt in the service
of love, because doing so will improve the quality of your
life. At the freemasons' funerals, there was much hurt.
And when people saw tears streaming down my face, they
probably assumed that those tears were a physical mani-
festation of my hurt. But they would have been mistaken. I
cried tears of joy knowing that the hurt I saw represented
how much those men were loved. More broadly, my tears
reflected the realisation that people are able to choose love
even though hurt is just a stone's throw away.

My tears of joy

Chapter 5 Tasks

Task 1 – Appreciating a special person in your life

I want you to think about the person in the world that you're closest to. And now imagine that they had died. If you manage to really picture life without them, then right about now, you'll feel upset. I want you to breathe in that feeling and think about why you're hurting (it's because this person means a lot to you). Now imagine that you were asked to speak about your special person at their funeral. I'd like you to make a list of the things that you love and appreciate about them on the notes page of your smartphone.

Sometimes we take for granted the people we love the most. We don't tell them how much we love them and why we love them. The person you wrote that list about is still alive, and that means that you still have the chance to tell them everything you love about them. So, in the service of loving connection, that's exactly what I'd like you to do. I'd like you to contact your special person and tell them how much you appreciate their existence on planet Earth.

Now, as you take the necessary steps to have this conversation, you'll have some difficult feelings. My guess would be awkwardness and nervousness. I

want you to embrace those feelings rather than fight
with them. Too often we get caught into thinking
that we need to defeat our feelings in order to be
able to do stuff. But that's not the case. Let me try
to make these ideas clearer with a metaphor often
called *Tug of war with a monster.*

> I remember a time when village celebrations would
> include a tug-of-war contest. Team A would hold
> one end of the rope, Team B would hold the other
> end and between the two teams there would be a
> large puddle of dirty water. The idea was to pull the
> other team into the mud. With that picture in your
> mind, imagine that you're in a tug-of-war contest,
> but that instead of being part of a team you're by
> yourself, and instead of pulling against another team
> of human beings you're pulling against a big, ugly
> monster. Between you and the monster is a large
> and seemingly bottomless hole. You start trying to
> pull the monster into the big hole, but when you
> look you see the monster chilling out, holding the
> rope with one hand while sipping a beer with the
> other. He just will not budge no matter how much
> effort you put into making him disappear.

Trying to pull the monster into the hole represents
the way you may try to get rid of your feelings of awkwardness and nervousness, in the hope that doing so
will help you to complete your task. This approach is
common to many of us when we have feelings that

we don't like. We try to pull them into a big hole so that we don't have to have them any more. But is it possible to do that? To avoid difficult feelings and still live our best life? And do we have to destroy our monsters in order to achieve the things we want?

The answer to those questions is 'No'. We can let our monsters exist and get on with the act of living. We don't have to destroy our unwanted feelings in order to thrive. By being accepting, we can learn to stop struggling with monsters. We can learn to let them be there. We can learn to drop the rope. It takes a lot less effort to do this, and when we stop fighting we can sometimes see that our monsters are not as scary as we first thought. In fact, we may see that they're not monsters at all – they're just the mind's way of trying to protect us.

How liberating could that be? To live a life where our difficult feelings are not the enemy, not something we have to fight with or change, but legitimate parts of our psychological make-up that we can simply acknowledge. Where our feelings are instead like a radio playing in the background – they exist, and we notice them, but they don't have to help us when making decisions.

Task 2 – Becoming a 'Yes' person

When we try to do many things that we care about, it's likely that we'll have to step outside our comfort zone. If you want to move forward with your career, you'll probably have to do interviews. If you're socially phobic but want a university degree, you'll probably have to work in groups. And if you want a romantic relationship, you'll probably have to go on first dates.

Whether we like it or not, uncomfortable feelings will often have to come along for the ride. Now, we might try to avoid them, and avoidance is reinforcing because it allows us to reduce our contact with discomfort in the short term, but when avoidance is our main priority, we're imprisoned by it. Willingness aims to circumvent the usual avoidance cycle by getting us comfortable with discomfort. However, as it can be tricky to undo old avoidance habits, I encourage my students to try a radical approach to jump-start their willingness training, and it's very simple. It involves saying *'Yes'* before saying *'No'*.

Have you seen the movie *Yes Man* with Jim Carrey? The film documents how a man's life changed when he started saying *'Yes'* to everything. It's a cool idea and pretty close to the way I began interacting with the world when I first learned about willingness. Of course, I differed from *Yes Man* in that if someone asked me to steal a pig from a farm and paint it green then I wouldn't say *'Yes'* (most of the time). However, whenever someone asked me to do something that was in line with what I wanted to achieve but that pushed me outside my comfort zone, then I said *'Yes'* straight away.

Let me tell you, it was one hell of a ride. Some of my *'Yes Man'* experiences are a little too extreme to detail here (if you ever bump into me in a pub then ask me about them) but what I can tell you about was the impact that it had on my education and career. From the third year of my degree, I got into a habit of saying *'Yes'* to every offer that was in line with my goals, especially when the offer made me feel uncomfortable. Yes to a PhD (even though members of the psychology department at Swansea University wanted to veto me beginning the programme after my performance as an undergraduate), yes to presenting my work at international conferences, yes to travelling to the US to meet renowned psychologists, yes to lecturing in Northern Cyprus, yes to writing my first book, yes to writing this book.

There's no doubt that I am where I am because of how readily I've said *'Yes'* to stuff that makes me feel uncomfortable. And taking this approach has built my willingness skill. Discomfort has become my good friend (in some ways I actively search for it because usually there's something important hiding there) and living this way has brought me liberty and fulfilment. Don't get me wrong here – willingness can be a hard road to travel, but it has opened up the world for me.

If you can carry your unwanted feelings with you then you'll be in a better position to step outside your comfort zone, and that's where the magic usually happens. So, for one week, I want you to become a *Yes person* and see where it leads. Anytime you're asked to do anything that pushes you outside your comfort zone you must say '*Yes*'. If you're asked to go on a night out with people you haven't met before, you must go. If a friend suggests you ask a potential partner out on a date, you must ask them out. If a course mate asks you to take the lead with a group project, you must lead. If your mum and dad ask you to accompany them for a walk on a nudist beach, you must take your clothes off and throw yourself into it. After a week, I'd like you to describe your experiences of being a *Yes person* on your notes page, and detail whether spending some time outside your comfort zone brought a different energy to your life.

Chapter 6

Practise Self-care

The danger of comfort zones

In the last chapter, we talked about how willingness could be a handy tool in helping us to step outside our comfort zone. And don't underestimate the importance of getting outside that comfort zone – this is where your dreams can come true. However, there's a caveat to this comfort zone thing that we have to consider. Specifically, if you spend too much time outside it then life can be stressful. In other words, although your newfound skill of willingness will help you to do things that make you feel uncomfortable, being in a constant state of discomfort will likely take its toll. We need an antidote to this dilemma.

Self-care, which involves doing certain things that keep us physically and psychologically well, is that antidote. What am I talking about here? It's very simple. You need to sleep well, and you need to eat well (in addition to your exercising habits from Chapter 2). These are the things that anchor us when life gets tough (and yet are often the first things to be thrown out of the window), and when these behaviours are combined under the umbrella of *self-care,* they're reliably found to predict physical and psychological health.

First out of the window are sleep, exercise and eating well

Back to basics

Let's start with sleeping. The importance of sleep is something I can vouch for given that my son has stopped me
from having so much of it in the last few years, but other
psychologists recognise its importance too. For example, I
have one psychologist friend whose first question to someone experiencing delusions is, *'Are you sleeping properly?'*
because, in their eyes, it's more likely that the delusions
will be occurring as a result of poor sleeping habits rather
than psychosis. Research tells the same story. Better sleep
quality (and not duration, incidentally) is related to better
mood regulation, motivation, quality of life and mental
health. What's interesting is that there appears to be a
bi-directional relationship between sleep quality and wellbeing. Specifically, low wellbeing causes poor sleep habits
and poor sleep habits cause low wellbeing. It's a vicious
cycle I wouldn't like to get into.

Your diet and nutritional habits are just as important,
with healthy eating associated with better psychological
wellbeing and cognitive functioning. You are what you
eat, as the saying goes. Even the likelihood of engaging in
anti-social behaviour reduces if you eat healthily (don't ask
me how this happens). It seems as though the important
foods to incorporate into your diet are Omega-3 fatty acids
(which basically means eating fish, but for those vegans
among you it can also be found in seaweed, walnuts, kidney
beans, flaxseed oil and hemp seeds) and Vitamin D (which
means eating more fish, but it's also found in egg yolks,

mushrooms and many fortified foods like milks, cereal and orange juice). Additionally, research has shown that too much consumption of Omega-6 fatty acids (found in chicken, eggs, nuts and breads) and too little consumption of folic acid (found in cereal, rice, pasta and breads) are both relevant to wellbeing.

To be quite frank, gathering reliable information about nutrition is a nightmare, as can nicely be illustrated by the fact that bread falls into both the Omega-6 and folic acid categories above. Conflicting research studies and big business biases mean that it's hard to make sense of it all (I know this because Amy and I took the decision to become vegetarian a little while back and we're still not sure if it's a good thing or a bad thing, based on the research we've read). However, there are some reliable things that you and I do already know, even if it's hard to admit it. Eating too much chocolate, crisps, cake, pastries and processed foods, and drinking too much alcohol, isn't good for us (I'm hoping you read that as quickly as I typed it). Therefore, even with the conflicting nutritional information out there, we can still take a big step forward by cutting down on those foods and eating more salad, fruit and vegetables. Unfortunately, if we don't improve our nutrition we may open up a can of worms. Not eating properly means increasing body fat percentage, and that means more physical health problems and potentially more psychological pain (in the form of health anxiety or even appearance anxiety).

Using our new skills to help us get this right

What's interesting is that many of us already know that taking care of our sleeping and dietary habits is important for human functioning, so why do so many people struggle to manage these basic aspects of self-care? The answer, as you well know by now, is the human mind. As we saw in Chapter 2, the mind is quite skilled at pushing us to do things that may not be in our best long-term interest. For example, if we want to reduce the amount of wine we drink, then our mind may tell us, *'It's been a particularly bad day today, why not have just one glass?'* Or if we want to break our maladaptive sleep cycle by waking up earlier in the morning, our mind may say, *'You deserve this sleep, why not just take that extra couple of hours now?'* Both of these examples have happened in my own life in just the last twenty-four hours, illustrating that even the *experts* aren't beyond these things.

So how do we get back to basics with regard to sleep and diet, with so much activity going on in our very human minds? My hope is that you already know the answer, because I've already told you it. However, if you've forgotten, then here's a recap of the major psychological skills that can help you to better manage the awkwardness of the human mind:

1. **Defusion** By becoming more aware of our thoughts, we can put ourselves in a position to spot them when they're being unhelpful. For example, can we relate in

a better way to a thought like, *'I'm never going to be able to get to sleep'*?

2. **Develop a flexible sense of self** Some self-stories will imprison us, so we need to hold them lightly. For example, can we interact more flexibly with a self-story like, *'I'm just not enough of a disciplined type of person to be able to eat more healthily'*?

3. **Willingness** Chances are that we want to eat that extra bit of chocolate because we're feeling down. Can we own that feeling and carry it with us? If we can, then we won't need to engage in what's essentially a short-term-fix avoidance behaviour.

Despite my best intentions, there's every chance that you'll not be able to call upon those psychological skills at a moment's notice until you've practised them a little more. In the meantime, I have two tips to help you get into good habits with regard to these self-care behaviours, which circumvent the need for the psychological skills I've just mentioned. Firstly, structure the environment so that it makes it difficult for you to falter. If you don't have wine in the house then it will be more difficult to drink it, or if you want to improve your sleep habits then invest in some blackout blinds and set loud alarms (that are difficult to switch off) at the times you need to be awake. Secondly, try to take part in activities that help you to self-care while also being enjoyable. For example, if you need to eat more healthily, perhaps consider signing up to a challenging cooking course that requires you to learn about new, exciting and healthy recipes. If you do this, then eating healthily won't be a chore – it will be a process that you enjoy.

Caring for our psychological self

At university, sleep and diet are pertinent challenges for you. For example, if you live in shared accommodation there may be people constantly disturbing your sleep, and if you haven't been taught how to cook at home (like I wasn't), then you may very quickly come to rely on foods that don't nourish your body (for me, it was curry, rice and chips from the chip shop). Or if you live at home, without a reason to get up in the morning, you may find yourself binge-watching TV series in the early hours and eating crappy foods while you do so. Wherever you happen to be, taking the time to get those things right will benefit you.

Something else that will benefit you involves getting better at caring for your psychological self. You see, looking after our sleeping and dietary behaviours, for the most part, concerns caring for our physical self. But caring for our psychological self is just as important and happens to be something we're generally very bad at. I'll describe and explore three personal situations to try to illustrate what I mean:

- **Situation 1** When I was in university, I set myself the challenge of learning to play the guitar. Although I tried for a little while, I ultimately gave up.
- **Situation 2** When Max was two years old, I left him at the top of our drive in his pram and went back to

close the front door. When I returned Max had rolled down the drive, his pram had flipped forward and he'd crashed face-first onto the pavement (I shiver each time I read those words).

- **Situation 3** When I was around fifteen years old, I witnessed a young lad get attacked by a group of bullies. They ended up hurting him physically and I did nothing to stop it.

Those situations might seem very different, but they're tied together in one important respect. Following each of them, I picked up a big metaphorical stick and hit myself with it. I did the opposite of caring for my psychological self; I engaged in self-criticism. And this is how a whole load of us respond to such failings. We tend to be our own biggest critics. In fact, people report that the majority of thoughts they have about themselves are negative (with some estimates between a shocking 75 and 90 per cent).

Have you noticed this? Have you noticed just how unpleasant our minds can be to us? They're forever finding fault, criticising, sneering, complaining and jumping to unwarranted conclusions. For example, when you look in the mirror, does your mind say, *'You look amazing'* or is your attention drawn to those parts of yourself that aren't quite how you'd like them to be? Or, when you think about the past, how often do you remember triumphs and successes versus times when things went wrong or times when you didn't behave quite as you would have liked?

Our minds have this incredible ability to berate us following events in our lives and when this happens,

155

there's actually double the amount of psychological pain. Specifically, in Situations 1, 2 and 3 above, there's the pain of the event itself (giving up, seeing my son injured and watching someone get hurt) and there's the pain of the self-criticism that goes with it, which often arrives in the form of unhelpful thoughts and unhelpful self-stories (*'You're such a loser for giving up, you've done this again and again', 'You're a bad father, you don't deserve your boy', 'What a terrible human being you are, letting some-one get hurt'*).

Practising self-compassion

While human beings can show amazing kindness, care and love for each other, we're pretty rubbish at taking care of our psychological self when we mess up in some way. What can we do about this? Based on the work of Dr Kristin Neff, I recommend a healthy dose of self-compassion.

Compassion is comprised of two distinct parts: it's about being sensitive to other people's distress and being moti-vated to do something about it. When we have compassion, we feel other people's pain and make efforts to support them with it. Self-compassion is essentially the same process, only it involves acting in this way towards ourselves. It involves noticing our critical minds, our pain or aspects about us that we don't like and responding with kindness, patience and understanding. As an alternative to relentlessly criticising ourselves for our inadequacies, we ask this question, *'What can I do to care for my self in this moment?'*

Sounds great, right? However, the trick is figuring out how to become more self-compassionate, as there's no magic wand. Luckily, there are a lot of exercises to help us to practise this skill which you can find online easily enough. The visualisation script below is one such self-compassion exercise that I particularly like. I want you to read it slowly, and to remind yourself of it when you mess up.

▲ Imagine yourself at eight years old. Think hard about what you looked like at that age and put that face into this exercise.

▲ Now think about what you might have been wearing on a typical day. Possibly a sports kit, possibly your school uniform, possibly a dressing-up costume. Let's go with your school uniform.

▲ Who would you have spent time with that day? Maybe you woke up in the morning and had breakfast with your mum, maybe your dad stole a mouthful of your porridge to make you laugh, maybe your mum then walked you to school.

▲ Think about what you would have been like in school. Maybe you would have played with your friends, maybe you would have been kind to another child, maybe you liked playing chasing games.

▲ Now picture your schoolyard. Imagine that you were playing a particularly competitive chasing game and that you were winning at this game. Imagine that you ran across the grass, then behind the trees, and then you headed to the concrete area. Picture yourself doing this, picture your hair flowing in the wind, your legs moving fast and a big smile on your face.

▲ As you enter the playground at this ferocious pace you trip on a stick. You fly forwards. You scrape your hands and your knees on the gravel. You see blood in various places. You feel pain screaming through your body and you begin to cry.

▲ Now imagine that time has stopped. Everything is still. Your eight-year-old self is on the ground. Your friends have started to panic. Your teachers are just being alerted to the situation. But time is still. There's no further movement.

▲ Now imagine that you, right now, in this moment, were able to go back in time and be the first person to speak to your eight-year-old self, following this event. What would you say? What would you do?

▲ You might pick up your eight-year-old self and give them a huge cuddle. You might tell them that it's OK to cry. You might cry with them as they feel the pain of the fall. You might take them inside to the first aid station and sit with them while the nurse treats their wounds. You might check on them throughout the afternoon and walk them personally to meet your parents at home time. You might go home to your friends after this and tell them how hard it was to see the child in pain, and how you tried your best to support and comfort them.

Flick back to the present moment, to the room you're currently sitting in. Why did I ask you to visualise that event? It's because, in some ways, you're still that child. You're still running through this world picking up self-inflicted bumps, cuts and bruises (you'll fail when pursuing goals, you'll make mistakes, and you'll act in ways that bring you shame). When you pick up these bumps, you'll berate and criticise yourself for being such an idiot. But let me ask you a question. Has self-loathing ever worked as a way to move forward positively in your life? In the long term, have you ever achieved more as a result of self-criticism? I'd guess not. Perhaps you could try something different? When you mess up, could you try to treat yourself in the same way that you would have treated your eight-year-old self in that playground?

In the three situations I described earlier my own mind picked up a big stick and beat me with it, where a little bit of self-compassion would have gone a long way. You're going to be no different from me. You're going to make some mistakes in your life, and some of them are likely to be whopping ones. Yes, you'll fail at challenges, but you'll also get too drunk and do something truly embarrassing, you'll hurt people's feelings without meaning to, and worse still, you'll hurt people's feelings on purpose in a way that eats at you afterwards.

When you make your mistakes, let me promise that beating yourself up won't improve the situation. Treat yourself kindly. You're a human being. You're not perfect. Give yourself a break. Provided you know that you wake up in the morning with the intention of being a good person then that should be enough for you to be able to sleep at night, irrespective of how you might get it wrong on occasion. That's my advice. Practise self-compassion. Try to extend the same kindness and support to yourself that you would give so easily to someone you love.

Digging for gold

That's not the end of our coverage of self-care or self-compassion. There's more analysis to do. I realise that we're about halfway through this chapter and therefore that this is prime time for nodding off, but try to stay with me here, because I need you to see that there's always useful information, or gold, in our pain that can help us to grow. I'm going to use the three situations again to illustrate what I mean. Although each one resulted in me beating myself up, the severity of the beating differed in each case. I want to explore this a little because it's important.

Situation 1 was a low-level self-beating. Essentially, I set myself a challenge and I gave up. Although I wasn't particularly happy about this, there were no major long-term consequences with regard to self-criticism. It might surprise you to know that there were also no major long-term self-criticism consequences from *Situation 2*. Don't get me wrong – at the time it was horrific. My son had blood pouring from various places on his face and the swelling made him look very strange. And it was my fault. I lay next to him for the whole night, listening to every breath to make sure that the bang to his head hadn't done some damage to his brain that might result in him stopping breathing. I didn't sleep a wink and I continually burst into tears, reliving the series of events and asking myself how could I have been so stupid? How could I let this happen when I'm the very person that should be protecting him? What sort of dad would let this happen to his son? Surely, I wasn't cut out to be a dad?

But although there was a serious amount of self-loathing at the time, it subsided pretty rapidly. Why? Because it was an event that I didn't choose to happen. I didn't mean for it to happen. I didn't do it on purpose. Although I engaged in self-criticism in the days that followed, and although I learned a lesson about leaving Max at the top of our drive, I didn't question myself, or my ability to be a good father, in the long term.

This brings us to *Situation 3*, which still haunts me to this day. A lad was getting beaten up and I did nothing. This situation is by far the worst and resulted in the biggest self-beating. You may wonder why. How can it be possible that I beat myself up more about this than I did about letting my son drop down a driveway in his pram?

The difference between the two situations was that in Situation 3 I acted in a way that I was ashamed of. I had time to help, and I did nothing. You see, back then I held myself to be the sort of person who would act with courage and who would protect and care for people when given the chance. Yet here I was not bringing those qualities to my actions. There was a sort of incongruence between who I wanted to be in this world and how I acted. And that's why the self-beating was so severe, and why I lost sleep over it. However, over time I've been able to see the gold in this experience that can help me to grow. Specifically, if living a life that's not in line with my *values* brings me pain, then living a life that *is* in line with my values could bring me meaning.

Putting values centre stage

Values are the answers to some of these questions. What qualities do you want to bring to your actions on this Earth? How do you want to treat people? What principles do you want to stand for? What standards do you hold yourself accountable to? In some ways, values represent us when we're at our absolute best. For example, I feel I'm at my best when I'm *teaching others, striving to be a better person* and *showing love and affection in my relationships*. On days when I bring those values to life, I go to bed a happy man. On days when I act in a way that's counter to those values, I don't feel so good.

Values are a key ingredient for wellbeing and the lovely thing about them is that they matter for everyone, irrespective of personal riches. That is, values concern *how we act*, rather than *what we achieve*. Let me give you an example. Imagine Kevin, twenty-nine years old, lying on his deathbed. He says to his friends, *'I won't have lived long but I have lived well. I went to the best parties, I travelled the world, I got my dream job and I met the most beautiful people.'* Sounds like Kevin had a wonderful life, which is great. Now imagine Corinna, twenty-nine years old, lying on her deathbed. Corinna grew up in poverty. She just about managed to get through school and got a job afterwards in a workplace that still employs her. She says to her friends, *'I won't have lived long but I have lived well.'* One of her friends, in a moment of misguided frankness, responds with, *'Really? Because you haven't travelled the world, you struggled in school, your boss treats you poorly and you haven't met anyone special.'* Corinna smiles and says, *'Every day I tried to treat people with respect, to care for others and to work hard. I'm proud of how I've held myself on this Earth.'*

If values refer to the concrete things we accomplish, then only a small percentage of people will feel satisfied when they're on their deathbeds. *Why?* Because life is tough and many things are out of our control. For example, I'd love to take my wife and son to Disneyland. However, as much as I want to make this happen, we can't go to Disneyland any time soon because of practical considerations and current circumstances that are largely out of my control (i.e., we don't have a lot of money and there's a scary pandemic changing the world as we know it). However, if values refer to bringing qualities of our choosing to our actions, then we all have a chance at living a values-led life. For example, what's probably underneath the desire to take my wife and son to Disneyland is a value of *having fun with the people I love.* Well, I don't need Disneyland to have fun. I can bring that value to life, in small and large ways, every day (today

163

it was a water fight in our back garden that I lost quite convincingly).

Values are about choosing who you want to be in the world. Doing this will change how you act in your average day in a way that will bring you fulfilment. It will help you to have more *patience* with someone you might snap at, it will help you be more *compassionate* with people who are suffering, it will help you to continue with *self-development* projects when you feel down, it will help you to *persist* for longer with tasks that are difficult, it will help you to *love* yourself and others more fully. When I was growing up, I learned a poem from a book that my grandma gave me. It went like this, *'It is easy enough to be pleasant when everything goes like a song but the man worth the while is the man that can smile when everything goes dead wrong.'* I think that sentiment is relevant to us. If we can live a life that's in line with our values as much as we possibly can, in this unpredictable day and age when so much can go wrong, then not only will we sleep more soundly at night, but the world will probably become a better place too.

Figuring out our values

OK, I'm going to assume that this is all making sense to you in an intellectual way. It's amazing, however, in an experiential way, how little clarity people can have about their values. Consequently, you're going to do a little exercise (notes page, smartphone) that has been adapted from *ACT Made Simple* (a landmark book written by Dr Russ Harris).

From the list of values below, I'd like you to record ten that feel the most important to you. Then delete five of the ten. Then delete two of the five. Good luck!

- ▲ *Acceptance* To be open to and accepting of myself, others, life.
- ▲ *Adventure* To be adventurous, to actively seek, create and explore novel or stimulating experiences.
- ▲ *Assertiveness* To respectfully stand up for my rights and request what I want.
- ▲ *Authenticity* To be authentic, genuine, real, to be true to myself.
- ▲ *Beauty* To appreciate, create, nurture, cultivate beauty.
- ▲ *Caring* To be caring towards myself, others, the environment.
- ▲ *Challenge* To keep challenging myself to grow, learn, improve.
- ▲ *Compassion* To act with kindness towards those who are suffering.
- ▲ *Connection* To engage fully in whatever I'm doing, and be present with others.
- ▲ *Contribution* To contribute, help, assist, make a positive difference to myself and others.
- ▲ *Courage* To be courageous, brave, to persist in the face of fear, threat, difficulty.
- ▲ *Creativity* To be creative, innovative.
- ▲ *Curiosity* To be curious, open-minded and interested, to explore and discover.
- ▲ *Encouragement* To encourage and reward behaviour that I value in myself and others.

▲ *Equality* To treat others as equal to myself, and vice versa.

▲ *Excitement* To seek, create and engage in activities that are exciting, stimulating and thrilling.

▲ *Fairness* To be fair, to both myself and others.

▲ *Fitness* To maintain my fitness, to look after my physical and mental health and wellbeing.

▲ *Flexibility* To adjust and adapt readily to changing circumstances.

▲ *Forgiveness* To be forgiving towards myself and others.

▲ *Freedom* To live freely, to choose how I live and behave, and help others do likewise.

▲ *Friendliness* To be friendly, companionable, agreeable.

▲ *Fun* To be fun-loving, to seek, create, and engage in fun-filled activities.

▲ *Generosity* To be generous, sharing and giving, to myself and others.

▲ *Gratitude* To be grateful for and appreciative of the positive aspects of myself, others and life.

▲ *Honesty* To be honest, truthful, and sincere to myself and others.

▲ *Humility* To be humble, modest, to let my achievements speak for themselves.

▲ *Humour* To see and appreciate the humorous side of life.

▲ *Independence* To be self-supportive, and choose my own way of doing things.

▲ *Intimacy* To open up, reveal, and share myself (emotionally or physically) in my close relationships.

▲ *Justice* To uphold justice and fairness.

▲ *Kindness* To be kind, compassionate, considerate, nurturing towards myself and others.

▲ *Love* To act lovingly or affectionately.

▲ *Open-mindedness* To think things through, see things from others' points of view and weigh evidence fairly.

▲ *Order* To be orderly and organised.

▲ *Patience* To wait calmly for what I want.

▲ *Persistence* To continue resolutely, despite problems, difficulties.

▲ *Respect* To be respectful towards myself and others, to be polite, considerate and show positive regard.

▲ *Responsibility* To be responsible and accountable for my actions.

▲ *Romance* To be romantic, to display and express love, strong affection.

▲ *Self-care* To look after my health and wellbeing, and get my needs met.

▲ *Self-development* To keep growing, advancing, improving in knowledge, skills, character, life experience.

▲ *Sensuality* To create, explore and enjoy experiences that stimulate the five senses.

▲ *Spirituality* To connect with things bigger than myself.

▲ *Supportiveness* To be supportive, helpful, encouraging and available to myself and others.

▲ *Trust* To be trustworthy, loyal, faithful and reliable.

Bringing values to your life

You should have three values noted down. These are your most important values at the moment (that *at the moment* bit is important because values change across time, so don't hold onto any of them too tightly). If you do things that are consistent with these values, then you'll notice a difference in your psychological health. Given this, I think you should write down some ideas for how you might bring those values to life. But before you do, let me give you some guidance.

Broadly speaking, once you know what some of your values are, there are two ways to bring a greater focus to them in your actions. Firstly, you can let values *trickle into your life* as and when the situation calls for it. In other words, provided that you know your values (it may be a good idea to leave reminders of them around the place) then you'll be able to call upon them in circumstances that you couldn't have predicted. For example, if you know that *patience* is a value of yours then you can call upon it when your friend turns up for a group meeting fifteen minutes late. In this situation, you couldn't have predicted the event but, because you were clear about your value, you were able to use it as a guide for your behaviour when it was needed.

The second way to bring a greater focus to values involves *setting goals that are in line with them*. Arguably, doing this is more powerful than letting values trickle into your life because it comes with built-in commitment. However, before we get into goal-setting, it seems important first to discuss the relationship between values and goals. The way that I best understand it is via this sentence: you can't tick values off a list in the same way that you could with a goal. As an example, imagine I had a value of *contribution*, and imagine one day I managed to develop a new project that would help people. When I wake up the next morning, the value of *contribution* is still present for me. I can't tick it off a list, as it exists independent of the concrete things I achieve. If that explanation didn't quite hit home, the popular *Compass* metaphor may make it clearer.

> Values are like a direction of travel rather than a place you can reach. On a compass, values would be represented by the words North, East, South and West. You can move in those directions, but you can never reach those places. Of course, along the way you could tick off some of the places that you've visited while travelling in a certain direction. For example, if you go west of Bristol then you'll reach Ireland. After you've visited Ireland you could tick it off your list. In the service of travelling west (value), you have visited Ireland (goal).

To be more concrete about this, if one of my values is to be a *loving friend*, then I can never reach that place. It's a value that will guide me probably for the rest of my life. However, there are goals that I could complete that would bring the value to life. For example, I might commit to texting my best friend every Thursday morning. That's one value-consistent goal, and the more goals that I complete that are in line with my values, the better my life will be.

Digging into our values

There are four more things to know about setting values-based goals.

First (as I said in Chapter 3) make them precise (so that you know when you've completed them). In order to do this, I quite like a goal-setting formula called *WWWW*. This stands for:

- What (will you do?)
- When (will you do it?)
- Where (will it take place?)
- Why (is this goal important?)

An example might be something like this, *'I will read one chapter of my course textbook, this will happen tonight, in my bedroom, and I'll do this because the value of learning is important to me.'*

Second, it's important to set positive, not negative goals. Define what you want to do, not what you don't want to do. While you might want to stop doing something, try to frame this positively. For instance, instead of, *'Stop missing lectures'*, you might set the goal as, *'I will attend the lecture, every Wednesday morning, in the lecture theatre, because the value of persistence/progression is important to me.'*

Third, don't worry too much about the size of the values-based goal. Often, we can get pulled away from doing things that are important to us because our goals feel like a mountain to climb, but even ticking off very small values-consistent goals will positively impact your wellbeing.

Fourth (and this is a biggy), living a values-consistent life isn't easy. Not only do we forget them when we're running the rat race, but they can also bring us discomfort. Our values and our vulnerabilities go hand-in-hand. Here are a few personal examples to illustrate what I mean:

- *Striving to be a better person* often means sacrificing personal goals.
- *Showing love and affection* in my relationships makes me feel exposed.
- *Being patient* involves me being less productive.
- *Progressing in work* requires me to do public speaking.
- *Learning* reminds me of how much I don't know.
- *Caring for others* means experiencing loss.
- *Working hard* means doing tasks that don't make me happy.

These thoughts and feelings of discomfort can sometimes be barriers for us; they can stop us from moving in a valued direction. Therefore, we're going to need some of the other psychological skills we've talked about to help us to move towards our values when it's tough to do so. Despite sometimes being difficult, the more we do live a values-consistent life, the greater our sense of fulfilment will be in the long term. So have a go at the following exercise, which is designed to get your feet moving towards some values-based goals. It's all well and good knowing what your values are, but they mean nothing if you don't act in a way that's consistent with them.

- ▲ On the notes page of your smartphone, write down a value that you want to bring to your actions.
- ▲ Now write a small and meaningful goal that reflects your value and try to complete it over the next week.
- ▲ Once you've completed the goal, be sure to record any thoughts and feelings that showed up before, during and after.
- ▲ Let's up the ante. Using the same value, write down a bold goal that you could complete to bring that same value to life in the longer term.
- ▲ Before you try the bolder goal, write down any barriers, both internal (thoughts and feelings) and external (practical issues out there in the world), that might stop you from completing it.
- ▲ Once you've completed it, record any thoughts and feelings that showed up before, during and after.

Hopefully you'll now be able to see (1) how easy it is to bring your values to life through your actions, (2) how it feels to do so and (3) how our thoughts and feelings can sometimes push us away from what we care about.

Values at uni

Having a good grasp of values will help you in one university domain especially: peer pressure. When I was your age, there was immense pressure on students from their peers to drink beyond their limits, and there was also scrutiny with regard to sexual activities. These days, I'm sure that alcohol and sex are still pressure points for students. However, I think you now have the added complication of drugs. It feels like universities are a breeding ground for drug culture. OK, let me level with you about these things. There's nothing wrong with drinking or sex in moderation, and even taking drugs from time to time isn't going to be too much of a problem (be careful, though). In fact, doing those things in groups can be part of the fun of university. However, my experience is that there's a fine line between having fun and doing something you feel uncomfortable about.

Let's think about how values can help here. Firstly, if you happen to be the person pushing someone to do something that they're uncomfortable with, is that the sort of person you want to be? Can you get better at spotting when fun has turned into something else? Secondly, if you happen to be the person experiencing peer pressure, can you use your values to guide your behaviour, even though it would be socially difficult to do so? The sort of values that might matter here are assertiveness, authenticity, courage, learning, health, freedom, responsibility and self-care. How do you think you'd feel if you managed to choose your behaviour based on the qualities you want to embody in this world? I think you'd have a feeling of strength, and I think that this feeling of strength would generalise to other situations in your life.

The peculiar thing about values is that, as evidenced earlier in this chapter, they were the very reason for my shame. I did something that was out of step with who I wanted to be, and that spun me into self-criticism. However, values also provide me with a road map to greater meaning and fulfilment; a double-edged sword of sorts that we all have no choice in holding. In the coming months, putting your values centre stage will improve your long-term psychological wellbeing.

The take-home

Taking days off work, seeing our friends, doing hobbies, taking long hot baths and weekend breaks are the types of relaxation self-care moves that are important for our wellbeing. Eating correctly, maintaining good sleep hygiene and exercising are even more important – they'll help us to be strong when we're up against it. I know that students are busy and that you may feel there's no time for such activities, but you need to factor them into your weekly routine in order to be able to attack the various other elements of your life.

In addition to those basics of self-care, we also need to care for ourselves psychologically when we've let ourselves down. Over the course of our lives this is going to happen a lot. Not only will we fail at many of the challenges we set for ourselves, but we'll also act in a way that brings us shame (this sucks, I know). When that happens, we tend to pick up a big stick and hit ourselves with it. We berate our character as being sub-human, we view ourselves as not being worthy of success or love, and we assume that we have broken morals.

It's important you learn how to protect yourself when

self-critical thoughts come along. Self-compassion, which involves showing the same love to ourselves that we would easily give to other people, is a crucial tool in our wellbeing first aid kit in this regard. Don't get me wrong – self-compassion isn't a free pass to do what we want, and it doesn't give us a guaranteed excuse for letting other people down – but it can be like a backstop that prevents the spiral into self-criticism that often happens after we mess up. If you can bring a little bit of self-compassion into your world it will be a much nicer place to inhabit.

The other thing that will make your world a nicer place to inhabit is putting values centre stage. If you can be clear about the sort of person you want to be on this Earth, and bring those qualities to your actions, then you'll be winning at life.

Chapter 6 Tasks

Task 1 – Keeping an eye on our buckets

There's a metaphor about human behaviour that I love. I'm not sure where I learned this one, but I find myself referring to it again and again. It goes something like this.

> Imagine that an empty bucket represents you. As you move through your life, different events happen that change the water levels in your bucket. For example, getting sacked at work, losing a loved one, cutting your finger on a cheese grater, having WiFi that breaks and not having enough money to pay the bills would be the type of events that would likely fill your bucket with water. Walking the dogs on a summer day, passing an exam, having a nice meal, being financially stable and speaking to loved ones, on the other hand, would likely reduce the water level in your bucket.
>
> As the bucket fills with your stresses and strains, it becomes heavier and more difficult to carry. Your tolerance for life's frustrations diminishes. Eventually, your bucket is full. Life has become too much. All that's needed is that final drop to push you over the edge, and usually that final drop comes in the form of a person in your environment who does something mildly annoying. Most of the time, the person causing the spillage has barely

contributed to the problem. Nevertheless, they will feel the full force of your wrath.

Does this sound familiar? Have you ever taken your anger out on someone who wasn't really deserving of it? If so, please answer the questions below on the notes page of your smartphone (I'll put in some model answers). The hope here is that you can use this metaphor to help you to behave in a values-consistent way during periods of your life when it would be easy to do otherwise.

Describe the situation.

My friends were making too much noise following a night out. My bucket was full because that day I'd failed an assignment. I flipped my lid with them in a way that wasn't acceptable.

How did you feel following it?

I felt horrible, and ashamed. The next day I could barely look at my friends.

How did you improve the situation?

I apologised, and when I did, I let them know that my anger wasn't really meant for them. It was meant for myself because I failed the test.

Did you experience self-criticism and how could you have better managed it?

I did experience self-criticism. Possibly a bit of self-compassion would have helped. I failed a test. I reacted by doing something I wasn't proud of. But I'm just a human being. I didn't need berating. I needed understanding.

In the future, is there a way you can stop this sort of thing from happening in the first place?

It's important to keep an eye on when my bucket is full so that I don't act in a way that's counter to my values. Therefore, following personal hardships, I'll try to be more aware of how my stresses and strains might spill over onto innocent people. If I can spot the days when I need to sit on my hands, then my hands can do less damage.

Lastly, what values do you think were underneath your self-criticism?

Respect for others, flexibility, connection and being a good friend are values that are obviously important to me.

One drop makes a full bucket overflow

Task 2 – What domains in my life are important?

The thing about values is that they exist across different domains in our life. Some of these domains will be more important to us than others, and it's very easy to spend more time than we'd like in domains that we don't really care about. Let's do an exercise, adapted from the work of Dr Kelly Wilson, to try to figure this out. Below are some instructions for how to complete the exercise but the easiest way to understand it is probably to flick to the table below where I've put in some model answers:

▲ Draw four columns on a piece of paper.
▲ In the first column, write the following words in each of the rows: Friends/Social Relationships, Family Relationships, Intimate Relationships, Work/Career, Education/ Learning, Growth/Self-development, Recreation/Leisure, Spirituality, Citizenship/ Community, Health/Physical Wellbeing.
▲ In the second column, put a number next to each domain ranging from 1 to 10. Lower numbers mean that the valued domain isn't important to you, while higher numbers mean that the valued domain is important to you.
▲ In the third column, put another number between 1 and 10. In this column, a lower

number means that you haven't given that domain much behavioural attention in the last month, while a higher number indicates that you have given the domain in question a lot of your behavioural attention.

▲ Finally, in the fourth column, write the mathematical difference between columns two and three. The higher the number in column four, the more of a discrepancy exists between the importance of a valued domain and how much behavioural attention you give it.

	Overall Importance (1–10)	Action (1–10)	Concern Score
1 Friends/Social Relationships	.6	8	-2
2 Family Relationships	10	5	5
3 Intimate Relationships	8	8	0
4 Work/Career	6	8	-2
5 Education/Learning	8	5	3
6 Growth/ Self-development	10	3	7
7 Recreation/Leisure	7	4	3
8 Spirituality	4	2	2
9 Citizenship/ Community	5	2	3
10 Health/Physical Wellbeing	9	9	0

OK, now let's answer some questions about the exercise (pull up that notes page and follow my lead):

Which areas were most important to you?

Family Relationships and Growth/Self-development.

Do you give them enough of your behavioural attention?

My score in the third column for both of those domains was lower than I'd have liked.

If not, why do you think this has happened?

My scores for Friends/Social Relationships and Work, in the third column, suggested that I'm giving more attention to those domains than I'd like to, and there's only so much time in a day.

How can you rebalance these domains in your life?

Setting values-based goals in these domains would go a long way towards helping, and leaving reminders of the importance of these domains will cue me to remember them when life is busy.

What could you do today to rebalance these domains?

I'm going to play football with my son, this afternoon, in my garden, because the value of fun is important to me in the domain of Family Relationships.

Chapter 7

Embrace the Moment

Mythical tennis player

It became something of a legend with my classmates. On occasion, you could hear murmurings in the hallways, *'Did you see that lad leave the exam after forty-five minutes?'* ... *'Someone said they saw him playing tennis while we were still sat in the exam hall.'* It was my second year at university, and I'd employed an absolutely classic revision strategy for some upcoming exams. That's right – I'd guessed at what topics I thought would come up and I'd only revised those topics. When I got into the two-hour exam, which was held in a quaint off-campus building surrounded by gardens and tennis courts (called *Patti Pavilion* for those of you who know the City of Swansea), the topics I'd chosen to revise were nowhere to be seen.

To begin with, as you might imagine, I was somewhat unsettled. But I came around pretty quickly because I'm one of those strange people who gets excited before exams. I'm lucky enough to have motivating thoughts like *'Let's do this'* go through my mind rather than destructive thoughts like

'I'm going to vomit'. And I needed such positivity in those moments to help me along, for one major reason: as this was the second year of my degree, the mark that I received in this exam would contribute to my overall degree grade. The exam questions were in front of me. The paper and pens were in front of me. I was convinced I was going to smash it. The exam invigilator said the all-important words *'You may begin'*. And then it all went to shit.

The first thing that bothered me was the clock. If there's one thing I can't stand it's the sound of a clock ticking away happily (I've removed clocks from every bedroom I've ever had to sleep in). The flashlight of my attention was pulled away from the paper and pens and exam questions in front of me. The next thing that bothered me was that a student at the far end of the exam hall seemed to be coughing a lot. For all I know, it was some sophisticated cheating technique, but it was really distracting. A related cheating technique, which also distracted me, occurred when people went to the toilet (to read information written on their leg). I'll never know how they got away with it; it was a two-hour exam and people were going to the loo after only ten minutes. Anyhow, my attention flashlight was again drawn away from what was in front of me like the Eye of Sauron was drawn away from Frodo (cheeky *Lord of the Rings* reference there). Another thing that bothered me were the exam attendants walking up and down the aisles. My flashlight often flickered onto those horrible creatures too.

That's not the end of it. My attention flashlight was also pulled away from what was in front of me by my own thoughts. Some of these thoughts concerned the past, *'You're such an idiot, why didn't you revise differently?'* or *'This is a lot like that time where you failed an A-Level exam.'* But most of the thoughts concerned the future, *'You're going to fail this exam and then your degree'*, *'How are you going to tell Mum and Dad about this?'* and *'The people in your class are going to think you're pretty dumb.'*

Back in those days, the earliest you could leave an exam was after forty-five minutes, which was exactly the point when I left this particular exam. I was the first person to leave. My housemates, by coincidence, had booked a tennis court right next to the exam hall for that afternoon. After walking out I went back to my student house, got changed, found my racket and went to play tennis. I'm not exactly sure what informed my decision to do this, but it would have been one of three things. Firstly, my friends were already playing tennis and maybe I didn't have a whole lot else to do. Secondly, maybe I felt rubbish and wanted to distract myself. Thirdly, I quite like being rebellious sometimes and so maybe this was a way to hold onto a rebellious reputation (given that I was sure to lose any academic one). When the people from my course left the exam hall some of them could see me laughing and joking on the tennis court, and hence the legend was born.

Being mindless

But don't be deceived by this story into thinking I was some cool maverick. The truth is that I was a big numpty from start to finish. So, what went wrong? Well, the first thing that went wrong was that I revised topics that didn't come up in the exam. It was an important lesson for me in exam strategy. But what went wrong during the exam? Despite my faulty revision shenanigans, I still had a chance to achieve something in that exam hall. Unfortunately, my attention flashlight was distracted by some things around me, and by some things inside me. My flashlight should have been directed, for the most part, to the paper and pens and exam paper on the table in front of me. If I could have managed this then I would have been able to embrace what was important in that particular moment.

If I could go back in time, knowing what I know now, do you know what I would do differently? I would have done some mindfulness practice in the months leading up to the exam. I can hear the shrieks coming from inside your head, *'Oh no, not that mindfulness thing!'* Yes, that mindfulness thing. Sure, mindfulness is annoyingly fashionable at the moment, no doubt about it, but that doesn't mean that it can't be useful. In this situation it would have been supremely useful, because one thing that mindfulness allows us to do better is to control our attention flashlight.

Your attention please

At the most basic level, mindfulness can help us to orient our attention back to what's important in the present moment when we've been pulled away. In that exam room, if I were more mindful, I would have been better able to notice my wandering mind and to refocus my attention flashlight on the exam, which would have helped my performance.

As with many of the other psychological techniques we've looked at in this book, you may wonder how you can become more mindful. Luckily for us, mindfulness is a skill. That is, it takes practice in the same way that learning a harmonica takes practice. The more we practise mindfulness, the better we'll be able to catch when our minds have wandered away from the present moment. There are lots of mindfulness exercises on the internet to help us practise (for example, there's a website called *Frantic World* that has some great recordings on it), but I want you to have a go, right now, at the simplest mindfulness exercise that exists: mindfulness of breath.

▲ Get yourself into a comfortable position and keep your attention focused on your breathing.

▲ Each time your attention is drawn away from your breath (to external things around you and to thoughts about the past or future), gently reconnect with the process of breathing.

▲ Do this exercise for three minutes and then write down some comments about your experience on the notes page of your smartphone.

How did you find that breathing exercise? I remember leading a mindfulness of breath exercise not too long ago during a stress-management intervention with teachers. My flashlight, as the *expert* leading the session, was easily drawn into negativity from the past (*'Remember the last training you did? It was terrible'*) and negativity from the future (*'There's no doubt that these teachers will get absolutely nothing from this, and you'll never be asked to come back here again'*). My mind wandered relentlessly. The teachers reported experiencing something similar, and as a result many of them evaluated themselves as being *not good* at mindfulness. But they were mistaken in this conclusion.

It's a common fallacy to think that if you can maintain your focus on your breath then you're good at mindfulness, and if you can't then you're rubbish at it – but mindfulness doesn't work like that. Being skilled in mindfulness doesn't involve reaching some Zen psychological state where you can maintain focus on a single thing for hours. Instead, it involves becoming more aware that minds easily wander, it involves becoming better at catching our mind when it has wandered, and it involves having more skill in gently reorienting our attention back to the present moment. Can you see now why this might have been useful for me in that exam hall?

A good metaphor for these ideas that I often tell my students involves trying to train a puppy to sit.

> If you try to train a puppy to sit then it will probably run off each time that you say *'Sit'*. We don't generally get angry or cross with puppies when they do this because they're just doing what puppies do. Our minds are like puppies (they keep running off to different places).
>
> People often think that the point of mindfulness is to train our puppy-like mind to sit and stay. However, the

real point of mindfulness is to simply appreciate that we have puppy-like minds that will probably be puppy-like forever. Once we begin to notice where our puppy-like minds wander off to (stuff happening around us, thoughts, feelings and bodily sensations), then we'll be in a better position to bring them back to, and spend more time in, the present moment.

Being a mindful student

There are loads of situations where having a stronger mindfulness muscle will be helpful in your university life. As an example, it can come in handy when trying to manage pre-exam stress, and the stress of assignment deadlines. *How?* you might be thinking. When revising for an exam or working on a report, being distracted means doing less work, and doing less work means getting more stressed. If you can get better at noticing when your mind has wandered away from the task in question, you can spend more time doing the thing you're meant to be doing (or being in *flow*), which will lower your stress levels.

It can also help you to learn more in teaching sessions. Let me expand. How often can you get through a movie without checking the socials on your smartphone? Yeah, I can see you smiling. Most people struggle to maintain their attention on an activity that they actually like to do. Now, let me ask you another question. How often can you sit through a one-hour lecture, an activity that's far less enjoyable than a movie, without checking the socials? Yeah, I can see you smiling. When I'm giving my lectures, I'm pretty sure that every person in the audience has checked Instaface at least one time. In other words, the flashlight of their attention has been pulled away from what was important in the moment (I mean important in the context of their values).

It's gotten to the point where if I catch my students on social media during our sessions, then the deal is that I get to update their status (e.g., *'Dr Nic Hooper is just wonderful. He even smells great'*). But even that threat doesn't work as a deterrent. My gut says that it's actually a lot worse than just social media. I reckon that a student's attention flashlight gets pulled away in lectures and seminars in loads of different ways, and on loads of occasions, and that they often leave a teaching session having only understood and retained about 10 per cent of the content. What a bloody waste of time.

And do you know what? I reckon the attentional challenges you face are going to be even harder in the world of online learning, where you can do no end of things while attending a teaching session. Developing your mindfulness skills can help you get more from university life.

Turning off autopilot

You get it, right? Mindfulness helps us to control our attention better. Simple as that. But let's answer a few other questions that often come up about mindfulness, in the hope that doing so will help you to get it even more.

Question number 1 *'What's with the breathing exercises?'*

I struggled with this too. Breathing exercises can sometimes conjure the image of a psychological guru, maybe a monk, usually sat on a pillow. And by conjuring this image, this thing that we all do pretty easily already can be transformed into a mysterious or magical skill that only enlightened individuals possess.

However, the truth of why breathing is chosen as the basis for many mindfulness exercises is much more boring. Simply put, breathing is always there (hopefully). No matter where you are in the world, if you find yourself in a situation where mindfulness might be helpful, then your breath is there to ground you. Now let me warn you that if you do manage to focus on your breath for a little while during a mindfulness exercise, then nothing too special will happen. That is, there's nothing inherently beneficial about focusing on breathing – you'll not turn into an enlightened monk on a pillow. But what you will have is an anchor, something you can return your attention to when your mind has wandered.

Question number 2 *'OK, so I understand a little more about why people practise mindfulness of breath, but I still don't get how developing meditation skills will help me in the real world?'*

The purpose of mindfulness practice isn't to get better at practising mindfulness exercises, as that would be pointless. The idea is that the attention-focusing skills you learn during formal mindfulness practice (like breathing and body scan exercises) will generalise to the real world (like during an exam). By the way, in order to help this gener- alisation occur, people often practise mindfulness during everyday activities (like walking, eating or showering) ... but more about this later on.

Question number 3 *'What's the link to mental health?'*

Good question. You would have noticed that mindfulness isn't just used to help people control their attention in exam halls. In fact, it's used mainly as a way to help people who are suffering with mental health problems (although, as an FYI, there's some evidence that people who have suffered from traumatic experiences should be careful about practising mindfulness without an expert present). The obvious answer as to why mindfulness is useful in this context is that when we spend all our time ruminating about the past or worrying about the future then our present moment isn't really a nice place to be. Mindfulness can help us to acknowledge such thoughts and feelings and embrace the 'now'.

However, there's more to it than that and it all links back to the notion of values that we talked about in the last chapter. Follow the logic here:

1. Mindfulness can help us to slow down and become better at noticing our thoughts and feelings.

2. Doing so will upset the sometimes automatic way that our thoughts and feelings lead to behaviour.

3. Therefore, if we can develop our mindfulness skills,

we'll be able to do a better job of choosing behaviour that's in line with our values.

4. And living in line with our values will help us to have better psychological health.

You see, human beings have a pretty cloud-like understanding of their own behaviour. In other words, like clouds, which are fuzzy and ever-changing, we often don't really know why we do the things we do, and we don't see how getting wrapped up in our thoughts and feelings can so quickly cause us to react. When this happens there's a good chance that we'll behave in a way that's counter to what's important to us and to who we really want to be in the world.

I'll give you a personal example of what I mean (I think I'm telling you this story because it's therapeutic to talk about the stress it caused me). Around the time that Amy was pregnant with Max, Dora decided that pooping on the kitchen floor in the middle of the night was a good idea. But that wasn't the worst part of it. Dora pooped on the kitchen floor in the middle of the night because she was hungry. You fill in the gaps. I'd wake up in the early hours of the morning to a horrible stench and I'd go downstairs to find half-eaten poops. I'd then have thoughts like, *'We should have left this dog in Cyprus'* or *'Amy is quite rightly going to want to give Dora away.'* My heart would beat at a ferocious pace and my blood would boil. Usually all of this would result in me shouting at Dora.

When broken down like this, it makes it seem that I was aware of the chain of events occurring in real time. However, that sequence happened so fast that I had no understanding of the way in which an event (Dora pooping on the floor) interacted with my thoughts (that we should have left Dora in Cyprus to fend for herself), my bodily sensations (increased heartbeat and boiling blood) and my behaviour (shouting). I was on autopilot and the result was a reaction that I wasn't particularly proud of.

I think the same can be said for lots of people. We bounce around in our lives with little awareness of what's going on, and we have no idea how to interrupt our automaticity so that we're better able to choose our actions. Instead of having a cloud-like understanding of our own internal and external behaviour, mindfulness aims to increase our awareness of the chain of events. It aims to help us pay attention, purposefully, in the present moment and non-judgementally to the world around us and to our own thoughts and feelings, so that we can live a life to be proud of. And if we do this then of course we're going to feel better about ourselves.

In sum, the more you practise mindfulness, the more you'll become aware of your wandering mind. The more aware you are of your wandering mind, the easier it becomes to bring your attention back to the present moment and to act with awareness, rather than react, in situations that matter. When it came to Dora, being more skilled in mindfulness would have slowed down the chain of events and allowed me to choose a behaviour that was more in line with my values. Shouting at animals – especially a former stray dog just worried about getting food – is not a behaviour that coheres very well with who I want to be when I wake up in the morning. (Note: if you're not a *dog person,* then I'd like to take this opportunity to apologise for all the dog stories in this book. You've every right to be thinking, *'Why does this joker keep talking about dogs?'*)

Time-travelling

Do you want to know something scary? Time moves in one direction only, and it moves proper fast. For example, I'm going to close my eyes and I'm going to wake up to find myself as a fifty-year-old man. My son is going to blink and when he opens his eyes he's going to be about your age, with a fifty-year-old dad. And before you know it, you're going to be my age, playing ludicrous and soul-destroying make-believe games with your young children. Recently, I was asked to say something at my cousin's wedding, and I really wanted to get across these ideas about the passage of time, so I wrote a poem. I'm no Dylan Thomas but see what you think of the first paragraph:

> *Though love is endless,*
> *the bodies that carry our love will fade.*
> *In fact, it is this part of being human,*
> *that makes us most afraid.*
> *But the days come and go and we forget about this,*
> *we forget about the passing of time,*
> *And we wake up old never appreciating a life,*
> *that now has passed us by.*
> *In the future when you are grey,*
> *you will yearn to re-live today's perfection,*

But you won't be able to,
because time moves in only one direction.

Not exactly a joyous message to be sharing at a wedding but the sentiment holds true. My grandparents would love to be the age of my parents again (living through the wonders of early grandparenthood and early retirement), my parents would love to be my age again (living through the wonders of early parenthood and career challenge), and I would love to be your age again (living through the wonders of freedom and exploration at university). Yet none of us can get our wishes. This is such a head-fuck for human beings. The fact that time has gone and we can't go backwards.

It's certainly a head-fuck for me, and it catches me out sometimes. Indeed, this happened only last week when I watched a movie called *About Time*. Spoiler alert. The hook of the story is that the male members of a family have the ability to go back in time and change the course of events. The main character uses this to his advantage, especially in the context of improving his success in romantic relationships. However, this film is really about the relationship between a son and his dad. There comes a point in the movie where the main character's dad passes away (the dad and the son were best friends, as I would like to be with my son). That wasn't too much of a problem for the main character as he could just go back in time and visit his dad at any point that he wished. However, soon the ground shifts (I won't tell you how) such that the main character can now make one last visit to his dad. When he arrives in the past, while playing snooker, both come to know that this is the last time they'll see each other. In response to this, the dad (who can also time-travel) asks the son to accompany him to another moment in the past. The movie cuts to about thirty years earlier, on an average day, where the dad and the son (who was now about ten years old) were simply running on a beach and throwing stones in the sea.

I was inconsolable. For the last fifteen minutes of the film and for about thirty minutes afterwards. Not just crying – I was sobbing so much that I couldn't get words out of my mouth. Amy must have thought I'd lost the plot (excuse the pun) and I couldn't quite understand the reaction myself. On reflection, I think the movie caused this emotional turmoil in me for two reasons.

The first reason concerns what I've already discussed, the heart-breaking nature of time. Currently, my son is five years old. Once he's six years old, I'm never going to interact with him as a five-year-old, ever again. I don't have the ability to go back in time and re-live events over and over like the characters in that movie. Experiences are lost, and there's something crushing about that element of life. What so many of us would do to go back in time and spend just one hour with someone we've loved and lost.

The second reason is that the movie provided me with an almost revolutionary message concerning my life. When the dad had the opportunity to choose any moment at all, he chose to return to what would have been just an average day. I would have done exactly the same. I would have returned to a day when I played with my son on the swings, or visited the local zoo, or dressed up as doctors, or played hide and seek. It's the average times, the ones that we often wish away, which are the best times, and this movie made me intensely aware that one day I'll lie on my deathbed trying to make a deal with the gods to take me back to the days that I inhabit, right now, with my son.

Do you see what I'm getting at? It's where I am right now that the future-me will long for, and there's a chance that you'll be no different. The word *embrace* translates into the word *hug* – therefore, embracing the moment doesn't just mean developing useful attention skills, it means using mindfulness to hug the present moment, with gratitude and curiosity, with the knowledge that there's a finite amount of moments in our lives. Having that message at the forefront of my mind helps me to throw myself into *Knights and Princesses* with my son, because I don't want to leave anything out on the field. This is such an uplifting message of hope, and one that continually inspires me to seize the day. And you'll be glad to know that I put these ideas of *hugging the moment* into my wedding poem also (it might have been quite awkward otherwise!):

However, there may be wisdom here,
now you know there's no time machine,
Let's think about it, for two lovebirds,
what could all of this mean?
It means living every moment side by side,
knowing that it won't come again,
It means exiting the rat race to pause and appreciate
   each other,

every now and then.
It means kissing, and cuddling, and holding, and giving,
It means connecting with such depth that you'll actu-
*   ally be living.*
Knowing that times moves on is melancholic,
there is no such thing as forever,
But knowing this also reminds you,
how special every moment is together.
May your days be full of light, may your nights be full
*   of peace,*
May your marriage adventure be filled, with a love that
*   doesn't cease.*

I know that life can be tough. I know that we can easily
get into the habit of wishing the days away, especially
when we're bogged down with coursework and exams and
working in low-paid jobs to pay the bills. I've been there
myself. But try to slow down, so that you can embrace and
appreciate the moment too. There's opportunity, every day,
to appreciate being where we are physically and psychologically, to appreciate the fractured beauty of our souls,
to appreciate the people who are special to us and the
situations we might find ourselves in. Trust me on this – in
the future you'll wish that you could go back in time to your
current self, shake them, and say, *'Grab this university
adventure with both hands! Look for the joy in every day!'*
To end this chapter, I want to say this. Throw yourself into
your experiences, whatever they are, and don't leave anything out on the field.

Hug the present moment, with gratitude and curiosity

The take-home

Imagine you arrive home from university and sit down at the table to start an essay. As you begin the essay, you send a quick text to a housemate asking about what the plans are for dinner. You then get back to the essay. A few minutes go by and you decide to retweet a cat video on social media. You get back to the essay. Next, you realise that the clock on the wall is ticking loudly, so you take it down and hide it in your friend's bedroom. After this, *Love Island* starts on ITV2. Exasperated, you accept defeat and give up on the essay.

Does this sound familiar? In this situation, you're struggling to control your attention. That is, the flashlight of your attention is jumping all over the place and isn't focused on the important thing that's right in front of you. Mindfulness can help with this; it can help you to bring your attention back, in a non-judgemental way (you're not abnormal for getting distracted), to what's important in the moment, and it can help you slow down so that you're better able to choose values-consistent action throughout your days.

But that's not the most important lesson in this chapter. In discussing the topic of impermanence (how time is finite), we actually moved a little closer to the Buddhist conceptualisation of mindfulness (and a little further away from a book that was meant to be a light-hearted exploration of psychological wellbeing ... sorry about this). For me, the passage of time is the single most complex thing for a human being to get their head around, and with time moving so quickly, we often fail to appreciate where we are right now. If you get a little bit better at mindfulness, you'll be able to spend more time in the present, and the more time you spend in the present, the more likely it is you'll be able to *hug the moment*, with gratitude and curiosity. So, attack your daily lives full throttle with the melancholic knowledge that time is ticking away.

Chapter 7 Tasks

Task 1 – Seeing things differently

There's beauty around us right now, if only we open our eyes to see it. This beauty exists in many different situations and in many different forms but the one that sticks out at a personal level is in the context of my relationships with students. For example, if, when a student is telling me about their distress, my mind wanders too much to thoughts such as, *'This is making me feel really uncomfortable'* or *'I'm not the right person to hear this'* then my flashlight is neither on the student nor the situation. However, when I control my flashlight a little better then I find myself in a place where I can really notice and appreciate (1) the beauty in the human being stood in front of me (usually they're in distress because they care about something and that's lovely to witness) and (2) the beauty of the situation (this person is letting me into their world). The bottom line is that it's impossible to see the beauty of what's in front of us if we're not psychologically present, and mindfulness can help us to get there.

I'd like to illustrate this idea for you, the idea that being more mindful allows us to better notice beauty. I'd like you to go for a mindful walk. Walking is an activity that we tend to do on autopilot, meaning that we often fail to see the beauty of what's around us. Your job is to walk a route that you've walked many times, and simply to bring your attention to the things in your environment. Every time your mind wanders away to any thoughts or feelings, gently reconnect with the experience of seeing the things around you.

Once you've done this, make some notes about your experience on your smartphone. My hope is that doing this exercise will help you to learn two things. Firstly, that when we're not mindful, we can easily miss the beauty that surrounds us in the present moment. Secondly, that mindfulness exercises can be done during everyday activities (in truth, we can be mindful in everything we do), and the more that you practise mindfulness in such activities, the better you'll be able to call upon that particular muscle when you really need it.

Task 2 – Hugging the moment

There's so much time in the day that it would be damn near impossible to hug every moment. In fact, it would be exhausting to try. Nevertheless, there are everyday moments that we may like to enjoy and appreciate a little more. Some examples for me might be the first time that I hug my son in the morning, my first coffee, answering emails that give me the opportunity to brighten someone's day, having a conversation with a good friend, going for a dog walk, reading a book, watching a film, eating my dinner, being with my wife.

Those are all events that I could easily take for granted and yet, at the same time, they're the nuts and bolts of my life and the moments that one day in the future I'll long to experience again. So, how can I go about pausing and fully appreciating such moments throughout my day? There's one really simple way that I find useful: three deep breaths. During such moments I take three deep slow breaths and inhale the wonder of my experience.

I'd like you to try this. Choose a day and through-out it take three deep breaths to help you to hug those everyday moments. Make notes about your experience of doing this on your smartphone. I want you to figure out if embracing the moment in this way has any positive impact on your sense of meaning and fulfilment.

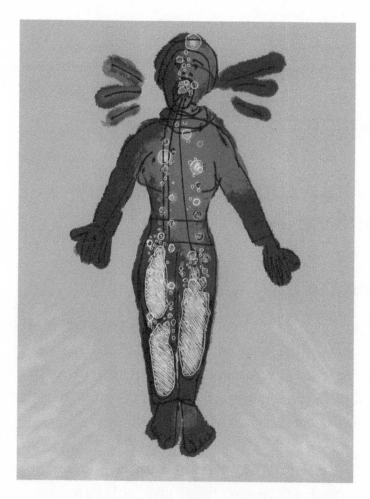

Take three deep slow breaths

Chapter 8

What You Need to Know Before We Part

Science, baby

Right now, you could well be mouthing these words at me, *'Only six rules, it can't be that simple?'* You'd be correct. Life isn't that simple and there's much more advice that I could give you. For example, here are ten other rules that popped out at me while writing this book:

1. **Listen to (but don't necessarily act on) your feelings** because they'll give you information about what brings you meaning and energy. As an example, remember when I described my reaction to Dora eating her own poop? Underneath my anger in that situation was (1) the fear of losing Dora and (2) the fear of stressing out my pregnant wife. When I listened, my feelings informed me that Dora and my wife were important to me (not in that order).

2. **Listen to other people before you talk.** Many people I know are too interested in their own opinion,

which means that they spend precious little time listening, instead formulating their own thoughts. Before you formulate, try first to listen. If you do this you'll pick up on non-verbal cues, you'll respond more appropriately, you'll develop relationships with depth and you'll learn about different perspectives.

3. **Try to understand that you need to earn your spurs** before you can be in a position to move upwards. What I'm saying is that at university, and in your future workplace, it's important to respect the people who are in positions of authority above you. Not only will they like you for it, but chances are there's loads of things you could learn from them. Although maintaining a critical mind is a good thing, I grew up being a bit too irreverent for my own good, and it never did me any favours.

4. **Don't assume that other people are always talking about you.** It's easy, as human beings who fear judgement, to assume that we're always being judged. The reality is that people are generally so wrapped up in themselves they won't even notice you. However, if you do find out that some person is speaking about you negatively then respond slowly because it's possible that (1) there's something to learn about your own behaviour based on the experience and (2) their own human history led them to that point, rather than anything in particular that you've done.

5. **Have fun.** A lot of this book is serious in nature because it's aiming to help you navigate your way through the trickiness of life. However, once you have these skills, they'll be a premise from which fun can grow. When your wellbeing is good, it's easier to see the fun in the situations you happen to find yourself.

6. **Play the university game.** The university game is simple: it means doing well on assignments. Therefore, what's much more important than actually attending your lectures and seminars is to know your module handbook, know your assessment deadlines, know the ins and outs of the marking criteria, and give yourself the time to write and then edit every piece of work you hand in, rather than taking a last-minute approach. Of course, if you're interested in learning then you'll love lectures and seminars, but if you're ever under a bit of pressure, remember that the way to win at the university game is to do well on your assignments. While we're swimming in these waters, I also think that you should get to know your lecturers (they mark your work) and get to know your classmates (you'll probably learn more from them than you will from your lecturers, and they'll be a more reliable source of emotional support).

7. **Don't get too wrapped up in social media.** Social media is wonderful because it facilitates connection. However, it's also awful. Firstly, it's addictive and as such can take us out of the present moment. Secondly, it provides a context for

comparison, which likely increases unhappiness. So be sure to control social media rather than be controlled by it. In addition, you may want to consider roping yourself into some good old-fashioned face-to-face socialising by signing up for a society or a club. Doing so will expose you to new people and new experiences that may bring you vitality.

8. **Don't apologise for thinking outside the box**, for brainstorming new ideas or for generally trying to push the boundaries of whatever world you live in. Often when people engage in such behaviour, others pull them down by asking questions like, *'Who do you think you are to think you can change the world?'* I believe the slang word for this type of a person is a *hater*. When haters come along, there's no *truth* behind their reservations. They're either trying to protect you from failure or they're going through some things themselves and are venting. Don't bite their heads off for doubting you – this is a mistake that I've made too many times.

9. **Respect money.** It's true that having money doesn't necessarily equate to happiness, but my experience is that having financial security will make a difference to your wellbeing. Don't get me wrong – I'm not saying you should spend all your time earning as much money as you possibly can – but I am saying that if you respect money throughout your life then you'll find yourself with less stress and more options for pursuing fulfilling activities.

10. **If and when you begin to have psychological troubles, speak to someone.** Heck, if you don't have a lot of people you can speak to then I don't even mind if you email me. Not talking about our problems not only perpetuates the idea that no one is suffering but it also isn't a great way to solve the problem. Other people, whether they're friends, acquaintances or a therapist, will give you a new perspective on whatever's going on for you, and you'll feel lighter for it.

Both you and I could add plenty of items to that list as we learn more about the nature of human beings on our journey of life. But what separates those bits of advice from the advice in the six main chapters of this book? Well, the information included in those chapters is special, in two important respects. Firstly, the rules are easy to remember (because they're so simple) and easy to apply (because they're so broad).

Secondly, and more importantly, the advice is supported by scientific evidence. We human beings generate knowledge in two main ways, based on our experience and based on science. The thing about science is that it tends to generate knowledge that's more reliable than the knowledge we generate at an individual level based on our personal experiences. What this means is that although those ten rules above may be useful, they'll not be anywhere near as useful as knowledge of the *Six Ways to Wellbeing* (or the other psychological tools detailed in this book), because they just don't have as much of an evidence base to support their effectiveness.

Now that you're an expert

As we're at the end of the book, you'll know lots more about the *Six Ways to Wellbeing* and *ACT* than you did fifty thousand words ago. This means that you're now ready to hear a couple more important details about them.

Firstly, the *Six Ways to Wellbeing* need to be chosen freely. To put this another way, the advice in this book will only have a positive impact if you make the choice, with autonomy, that making changes to your wellbeing is important and that adopting the *Six Ways to Wellbeing* framework seems like a good strategy for guiding you. If you engage in these behaviours because someone told you that you had to (or even because of an internal pressure like guilt), then you'll be doing them for the wrong reasons, and you'll give up quickly. Therefore, if you do use this book as your wellbeing guide, always try to connect with *why* it's important for *you* to do this. That is, if *you* have better wellbeing, then what will *you* be able to do more of during your time on planet Earth?

There's one other thing to say about this idea of choice. You get to choose *how* to bring the six ways to life. In the domain of exercise, for example, you get to choose dancing, fencing or gym work. In the domain of challenge, for example, you get to choose learning a new language, learning how to fix a car or learning how to paint. I won't go on, but you get the point: the choice of *how* to bring the *Six Ways to Wellbeing* to your life lies with you, and only you.

Secondly, although this book has broadly been written so that every chapter has a way to wellbeing and an ACT principle, everything is much more flexible than that. What do I mean here? Well, you can use any ACT principle across any of the *Six Ways to Wellbeing*. Let's take the areas of *Exercise (where we covered defusion)* and *Challenging yourself (where we covered self-stories)* as examples. You could draw upon *Willingness* when exercising (if you begin to feel physical pain) and when taking on challenges (if you struggle with the fear of failure). Or you could think about the *Values* that sit underneath exercise and challenge in order to persist when things get tough.

The other source of flexibility concerns how the *Six Ways to Wellbeing* can overlap. For example, my challenge in Chapter 3 was to learn to dance. However, learning to dance could also count as exercising behaviour. I actually achieved two things at the same time. If only for reasons of efficiency, you may want to think about this when bringing these well-being behaviours to your life. In sum, though, do view the various tools in this book as tools that you can use flexibly.

The story behind the story

I guess you might be wondering what set me on this book-writing adventure in the first place? It's quite the convoluted story but I reckon you'll like it. On the day of my son's second birthday, Max and I watched a film together. That film was called *The Lion King*. I'm going to assume you know what happens in this film, but one particular scene broke me, emotionally speaking. The daddy lion, Mufasa, died (well, he was actually murdered by his brother, but that's not the point). I'm sure that Max won't remember but I couldn't hold back my tears when I watched this scene. I cried because, in a moment of frightening clarity, I was reminded that life is unpredictable. That is, if Mufasa could die then I could die also (hopefully not in the same way). If that happened, then, as Max grew older, I wouldn't be there to guide him. I began writing a book to my son the very next day and called it *Dear Max*. My wife was under strict instruction to give Max this book at eighteen years old if I should happen to be maggot food at that time.

However, just because I was motivated to write a book after watching an animated children's movie doesn't mean that I'd have anything good to say. Most people, in fact, when I've told them about this endeavour, say something like, *'How did you know what to write?'* Well, that was easy for me, and it all began with *Sarah*. Remember her? If not, have a read through the first few paragraphs of Chapter 1 again. I was in Sarah's room. It was a couple of hours after I'd arrived. We were sat opposite each other holding a nice cup of coffee, and in this situation, I didn't quite know what to say. But I began speaking nonetheless and, inspired by the work by Dr Geetanjali Basarkod and the New Economics Foundation, described to Sarah the sort of things that psychologically healthy people tend to do. You may recognise these: Exercise. Challenge. Connect. Give. Self-care. Embrace.

The truth is that Sarah was lonely. She missed her home (parents and others), she had made no friends at university, and while all the people around her seemed to be finding romance, Sarah had no one. I think this feeling of loneliness is a common experience for students and if you've ever gone through this, I'm very sorry about that. It's a rubbish feeling. I've been there. I get it. I get what it is to be surrounded by people and yet still feel alone. I hope things have changed for you but, if not, then perhaps you might find this next bit helpful.

Sarah and I talked about how to apply the *Six Ways to Wellbeing* in a way that might address this feeling of loneliness, and this is what we came up with. Sarah made a plan to join the hockey club (Exercise), take a cooking class (Challenge yourself), apply to work for a drug addiction charity (Connect with people), volunteer at a shelter for dogs (Give to others), visit family as often as possible (Self-care) and practise looking for beauty in the here and now (Embrace the moment).

It was a great conversation because it gave Sarah a concrete place to start. However, there had to be more. Why? Because lots of people in the world make plans like the ones Sarah made and yet don't follow through with them. The reason for this is that their minds get in the way, so I needed to provide Sarah with a way to manage unwanted thoughts and feelings. The best way to do this, according to my research, was to teach her techniques derived from the latest advances in clinical psychology.

Sarah's loneliness

1. *I taught Sarah about defusion.* As she approaches
    activities, could she step back from unhelpful
    thoughts?
2. *I taught Sarah about self-stories.* Which stories
    were likely to stop her from completing goals and
    what could she do about it?
3. *I taught Sarah about willingness.* If she experienced
    horrible feelings while completing those activities,
    could she carry those feelings in her pocket?
4. *I taught Sarah about mindfulness.* In situations
    that matter, if her mind wanders to the past or to
    the future, could she bring her attention back to the
    present moment?
5. *I taught Sarah about values.* Could she use values as
    a guide for her behaviour when it would be easier not
    to?
6. *I taught Sarah about self-compassion.* When she
    messes up, could she give herself a break?

I left Sarah with three simple instructions that I'd learned
from mentors of mine over the years. *Be open. Be present.
Do what matters.* Sarah used this information to crack her
world right open. In a matter of weeks, she no longer felt so
distant from her family, and she no longer felt like she didn't
have any friends at university. The romantic relationship
thing didn't quite fall into place while I was in contact with
her, but I think that makes sense, as romantic relationships
tend to be the stuff of serendipity. That is, other than putting yourself out there, there's very little that anyone can

do to force this type of human connection. Until it happens, you sort of have to accept that this is the case and still live every moment to the full (and Sarah now had the skills to do this).

The success that I had with Sarah led me to teach countless other students about these things, and consequently, when it came to creating my book for Max, I knew exactly what to say: (1) my chapter titles, in a book about wellbeing, needed to be these six behaviours that people with optimal wellbeing tend to practise a lot. I essentially needed to write a book that inspired him to do these things more. And (2) I had to teach him about ACT as a way to manage his thoughts and feelings. Not only does ACT have loads of research evidence showing it to be useful (I know this because I wrote a dull book about ACT research) but ACT has made me who I am today. Knowledge of defusion, having a flexible sense of self, the role that our history has in making us who we are, willingness, mindfulness and values, has helped me to push the boundaries of my existence, by allowing me to interact in a more useful way with my own thoughts and feelings. I hoped that some of these skills would create the same magic for Max.

I finished the book after a couple of years, and I was absolutely delighted. However, when I sat down to read it, I noticed something curious. My book wasn't only written to my son. Our life experiences don't happen in a vacuum. In the daytime, I was helping university students with their struggles. And then when I went home, I was writing a book designed to help my son with his struggles, that was to be given to him when he was the age of a university student. It turned out that I was writing the book not just to Max as an eighteen-year-old, but to Sarah, and to every other student that I'd ever spoken to about these things. And that was the point at which *Dear Max* became *The Unbreakable Student*.

This means that you're essentially reading advice that I'd be giving to my own son in the event of my death (sorry for the morbidity here). However, some changes had to be made to *Dear Max* because that original version was deeply individualised (Max will still receive the only copy of this when he's eighteen). I therefore spent a lot of time thinking about how best to rework the book so that it would be more palatable to students. The answer for how to do this came from my teaching experience, and specifically this idea: the degree to which students take on my advice depends a lot on my relationship with them. Those who view me as a trusted, genuine, entertaining and credible gentleman tend to listen to me. But how do I achieve that position when I teach? Well, I make it personal. I tell my students about me and my life and, as a result, students connect with me as a fellow human being, see me as someone who wants the best for them, and therefore trust me when I tell them stuff.

I've used that same principle in this book. I poured myself into it because I needed you to *see* me, as an authentic and real human being, so that you'd listen to my advice. I hope this strategy has worked. I hope you feel you know me as a result of my writing and I hope, based on that, you know what an honour it is for me to have you read my words.

My final take-home

I'm currently sat in my kitchen, with a beer, trying to figure out what message I really want to leave you with. Here goes. People think that happiness is something we can control. But how can this be? If we could control happiness, then we'd be able to click our fingers and just be happy. But that doesn't happen. Why? Because the world can be a difficult place to live in. People get sick (now more than ever with Covid-19 at large), people die, people lose their jobs, people get their hearts broken, people struggle to feed their families and people struggle to maintain important relationships amongst a host of other hurtful events that can emerge during our time on Earth. People suffer. Even if everyone you see seems fine, the reality is that most people aren't (and I include myself in that category). Unfortunately, you'll be no different.

But here's a funny thing that not many people understand. There's nothing wrong with suffering by itself – it's a normal human experience. What is problematic, however, is when we respond to suffering in unhelpful ways. That is, we often try our best to *not* have it by doing things designed to help us run away from our feelings. This could be drinking lots, shutting down people, working extra hard, doing drugs, etc. This idea was summed up nicely in a TV programme called *Letter for a King*, where a wise character said, *'It's not the pain which ruins us, my child. It's the things that we do to avoid the pain.'* I'm here to tell you that you don't have to avoid your pain, you don't have to become embroiled in a war against your own thoughts and feelings. You can just have them and, at the same time, engage in these six important wellbeing behaviours while moving your feet towards your values. If you can do that then, according to my definition of the word, you'll be *unbreakable*.

You'll be unbreakable

In fact, not only is suffering not an enemy that you need to get rid of, but understanding and being familiar with the nature of suffering may actually be a great ally. Follow my logic here. Out of the *Six Ways to Wellbeing*, giving your love to other human beings is the single most powerful reason to be alive. If you know the nature of suffering (that it isn't something that you have to run away from, in either yourself or in other people) you'll provide anyone that you ever meet with a space that honours their very human pain. Think about how that will bring you close to people. Think about how it will better allow you to do the most important thing on Earth: love.

That might even be the most important message in this book. We're not alone in our pain; what humanity most has in common is, in fact, suffering, but suffering need not stop us from loving. So, love wholeheartedly, with energy, with compassion, with humour, with humility and with sincerity, even when it hurts you to do so. Yes, you'll need to work hard, yes, fate will play its part, but if you manage to suffer and still love in the way I've described, then the world is yours and you'll do a good job at this thing called life.

Thank you for reading my book. You've now reached the end, which means that I've taught you the most important wisdom that I have to teach. This wisdom has helped me to reach for the stars and prove the impossible. Now I want you to go and do what seems impossible too. Mark Twain once said that, *'The two most important days of your life are the day you were born and the day you find out why.'* I think I was born to write this book to you. I wonder why you were born and, therefore, what excitement lies in your future.

Chapter 8 Tasks

Task 1 – Reflecting on the journey

Pull up that notes page from your smartphone and reflect on the journey you've taken in reading this book. Answer the questions below in as much detail as you can to help you do this:

- What has stuck with you?
- What are the most important messages you've taken from it?
- Do you view yourself, other people and the world differently? If so, how?
- Do you feel happy that you've read this book? If so, why?
- How will this book change how you act in the world?

Task 2 – Looking forward

Now that you've looked backwards, I want you to look forward to the future by considering what you want your life to be about, and how you're going to get there. Have a stab at these questions:

- What do you really want from your life?
- What do you want to achieve in the next year/ three years/five years?

- What will you need to do in order to be able to achieve those things?
- What barriers are going to get in the way?
- What are you going to do when stuff doesn't work out?
- How do you want to treat people daily?
- How are you going to change the world?
- How can this book help you to do that?

Further Reading

I've drawn upon many resources in putting this book together, and I'd like to list a few of the more important ones here in case you're interested in reading further. The people who created these resources are psychology professors and clinical psychologists.

1. Geetanjali Basarkod's PhD thesis details how the 'Six Ways to Wellbeing' are predictive of good psychological health. In that thesis, you'll also see reference to many of the research studies I've described in the book. The thesis is available freely via the Australian Catholic University website.

2. Steven Hayes, Kelly Wilson and Kirk Strosahl wrote the first ACT book in 1999 (and a 2nd edition in 2016). This book, entitled *Acceptance and Commitment Therapy: An Experiential Approach to Behaviour Change*, will introduce you to many of the ACT principles described in the book.

3. A more reader-friendly ACT book you may want to

consider buying is called *The Happiness Trap* and was written by Russ Harris.

4. If you're interested in delving into self-stories in more detail, then my PhD supervisor Louise McHugh (with colleagues) has written a couple of books on perspective-taking from an ACT position. With a simple internet search, you'll find books that specialise in each of the other ACT processes too.

5. ACT is an evidence-based therapy and I know this because I wrote a book about it. If you're interested, then the title of that book is *The Research Journey of Acceptance and Commitment Therapy*.

6. If you want to learn more about persuasion, then the book that informed a lot of my words is called *Influence* and was written by Robert Cialdini.

7. If you'd like to investigate self-compassion a little more, then the works of Dennis Tirch, Laura Silberstein and Paul Gilbert are well worth looking up, as is any self-compassion book written by Kristin Neff.

8. Finally, if you want to know more about mindfulness, then search for books written by Jon Kabat-Zinn.

If you have any other questions about the research I've described, then do email me and I'll send over the reference.

Acknowledgements

Jaime Marshall: more than any other person, this book wouldn't exist without you. You've made me a better writer and your unconditional belief in my abilities carried me when I questioned whether I was worthy. I'm proud to call you my agent and my friend.

In addition to Jaime, other notable valued colleagues have supported me on this journey. Russ Harris was the first person to suggest that my writing voice would lend itself well to a book. Joe Oliver took the time to recommend me to Little, Brown Book Group. And Elaine Kasket has proven to be a wonderful mentor.

I'm also truly grateful to those who have helped with the publishing process. Andrew McAleer (Editor) has shown nothing but positive energy, support and confidence in myself and the project. Rebecca Sheppard (Production Editor) has shown efficiency and organisation. Sue Viccars (Copy Editor) has shown precision and attention to detail. And JP Flintoff (Illustrator) somehow managed to create illustrations that matched perfectly the tone of the book. *The Unbreakable Student* is far better for all your input.

Outside of *The Unbreakable Student*, a number of colleagues have shaped and continue to shape me. I'm incredibly grateful to the inspirational figures of Kelly G. Wilson and Steven C. Hayes, who gave me their hearts and their minds when I was but a graduate student. Louise McHugh was, in some ways, the first person to take a punt on me, and she helped me to achieve more than I ever thought was possible. Finally, in Freddy Jackson Brown, Duncan Gillard and Corinna Grindle, I have three colleagues who believe, as much as I do, that anything is possible, and having them in my life motivates me to keep pushing.

Not many people will know that I finished writing the book three months early because I wanted to run it by some of my students, friends and colleagues before submission. The feedback those beautiful human beings provided me with was an invaluable part of this journey. The names of those reviewers (not including some of the people above) are Mo Islam, Mei Ho Knit Chong, Harry Mansfield, Narik Dubash, Michelle Marchant, Chloe Oldfield, Kevin Walsh, Robert James, Gareth Delve, Harrison Rose, Olivia Church, Charlotte Rose, Adrian Fardini and Geetanjali Basarkod. (Note: you may recognise these names from the book, as they were used in all of my examples!)

Now down to the final few. I've always said that feedback in Academia is a bi-directional process. I'm thankful to my students at University of Kent, Middle East Technical University (Northern Cyprus Campus), Warwick University and University of the West of England for equipping me with the skills and experience to be able to write this book. Mum and Dad, you've given me everything, and Amy, you're the love of my life. Last but not least, Max. On the day you were born, my life became about being a good dad. Luckily for me, being a good dad to a kind, caring, thoughtful, funny and infectious little ray of sunshine is an easy thing to do – I hope we stay best friends forever.

Index